An Official Publication of The Napoleon Hill Foundation

POSITIVE INFLUENCE

NAPOLEON HILL

© Copyright 2022 – Napoleon Hill Foundation

All rights reserved. This book is protected by the copyright laws of the United States of America. No part of this publication may be reproduced, stored in or introduced into a retrieval system, or transmitted, in any form or by any means (electronic, mechanical, photocopying, recording or otherwise), without the prior written permission of the publisher. For permissions requests, contact the publisher, addressed "Attention: Permissions Coordinator," at the address below.

Published and Distributed by
SOUND WISDOM
PO Box 310
Shippensburg, PA 17257-0310
717-530-2122

info@soundwisdom.com
www.soundwisdom.com

While efforts have been made to verify information contained in this publication, neither the author nor the publisher assumes any responsibility for errors, inaccuracies, or omissions. While this publication is chock-full of useful, practical information, it is not intended to be legal or accounting advice. All readers are advised to seek competent lawyers and accountants to follow laws and regulations that may apply to specific situations. The reader of this publication assumes responsibility for the use of the information. The author and publisher assume no responsibility or liability whatsoever on the behalf of the reader of this publication.

The scanning, uploading and distribution of this publication via the Internet or via any other means without the permission of the publisher is illegal and punishable by law. Please purchase only authorized editions and do not participate in or encourage piracy of copyrightable materials.

Jacket design by Eileen Rockwell
Text design by Terry Clifton

ISBN 13: 978-1-64095-317-8
ISBN 13 eBook: 978-1-64095-318-5

Previously titled: *Napoleon Hill's 1947 Lecture Series*

For Worldwide Distribution, Printed in the U.S.A.
1 2 3 4 5 6 / 26 25 24 23 22

Contents

PUBLISHER'S PREFACE
1

INTRODUCTION
By Dr. J.B. Hill
Grandson of Dr. Napoleon Hill
5

PREFACE
By Don M. Green
Executive Director of The Napoleon Hill Foundation
11

CHAPTER ONE
Definiteness of Purpose | May 14, 1947
25

CHAPTER TWO
Master Mind | May 21, 1947
55

CHAPTER THREE
Going the Extra Mile | June 4, 1947
81

CHAPTER FOUR
Applied Faith | June 11, 1947
109

CHAPTER FIVE
Self-Discipline | June 18, 1947
131

CHAPTER SIX
Cosmic Habit Force | June 25, 1947
155

AFTERWORD
The Importance of Annie Lou, Napoleon Hill's Last Wife
199

Publisher's Preface

The book you are about to read is a transcription of six lectures delivered by Napoleon Hill in Los Angeles in 1947. The audience was comprised of people who were interested in becoming instructors of Napoleon Hill's principles, and others who were simply interested in improving their own lives.

Those of you who are familiar with Napoleon Hill know that he spent twenty years of his life interviewing the most successful men in America in order to write the first book on the science of personal achievement. In the course of his studies, he developed seventeen success principles. These lectures each deal with one of them. In order, they are Definiteness of Purpose, the Master Mind Alliance, Going the Extra Mile, Applied Faith, Self-Discipline, and Cosmic Habit Force. Hill often referred to these as the most important of the success principles.

Hill and his last wife, Annie Lou, established the Napoleon Hill Foundation 1962, and it continues today to publish his books, videos, audios, and lectures. These six lectures were transcribed but never before published and only recently found by the Foundation. The Trustees of the Foundation have chosen the title *Napoleon Hill's Positive Influence* for this book because these lectures deal with many of the influences that help people to become successful, and which drove Hill to achieve his own successes.

One of Hill's greatest influences was business tycoon Andrew Carnegie, who commissioned him in 1908 to undertake his twenty-year investigation. During his investigation, he discovered that important positive influences on successful people included having self-discipline, learning from adversity, working in harmony with others, selecting "pace makers," surrounding oneself with positive books and mottos, being guided by Faith and what Hill called "Infinite Intelligence," social and physical heredity, and the law of Cosmic Habit Force, by which one's habits become ingrained in one's personality and character. All of these positive influences are covered in these lectures.

In addition to Andrew Carnegie, a number of individuals were positive influences in Hill's life, and they too are discussed in the lectures. Those whom he knew personally and who are referenced in the lectures include Thomas Edison, Henry Ford, Franklin Roosevelt, Mahatma Gandhi, Dr. Elmer Gates, Alexander Graham Bell, and Edwin Barnes. On a more personal level, he speaks fondly of his stepmother and his wives who helped him with his endeavors. We are fortunate to be able to present an introduction to the book by Napoleon's grandson, J.B. Hill, and a preface by Napoleon Hill Foundation Executive Director Don M. Green, both of which explain the important roles played by these women in bringing positive influences to bear on his life and work.

We hope you will enjoy and benefit from this newly discovered treasure trove of *Napoleon Hill's Positive Influence*.

Introduction

By Dr. J.B. Hill

The women in Napoleon Hill's life had a profound influence on his long and colorful career. He was born Oliver Napoleon Hill on October 26, 1883, in rural Wise County, Virginia. When he was eight years old, his mother died. Sarah, Napoleon's mother, married at age 16 and was 24 years old when she died.

Napoleon's father remarried a year later, and Napoleon's stepmother had a tremendous influence on his life. She was an educated woman, the daughter of a doctor and the widow of a high school principal. Napoleon often quoted Abraham Lincoln by saying, "Everything that I am or ever aspired to be, I owe it to my dear stepmother."

We often read about the negative aspects of Napoleon Hill's failed marriages, and I have firsthand knowledge of one of them. But there is another perspective on these "failures" that shows their positive effects. Each marriage resulted in amazing accomplishments in Napoleon's life.

Napoleon Hill's *Positive Influence*

Napoleon's marriage to my grandmother in 1910 was the result of an ad he posted in a Washington, DC, newspaper. The ad said, "An educated refined young businessman who just moved to Washington would like to meet a refined young lady." This marriage produced three sons, Blair, James, and David. David spent his career in the United States military, serving in World War II and the Korean War. He was awarded many honors for serving in the Army Air Corps during World War II and the infantry in the Korean War. He was awarded two silver stars, the Bronze Star, the Purple Heart, the distinguished Flying Cross, and eleven air medals, one for every five combat missions. He died at age 89 and was buried with full military honors in Arlington National Cemetery. He was my father.

I followed in my father's footsteps and served in the United States Marines for 26 years. After retiring from the military, I decided to attend medical school, and I am still practicing medicine today. I also serve as a member of the Napoleon Hill Foundation Board of Trustees. Other descendants of Napoleon Hill became doctors, dentists, bankers, and other professionals, all dedicated to making this world a better place in which to live.

After Napoleon Hill's divorce from Florence, my grandmother, he had a short marriage to Rosa Lee Beeland. During this marriage, Napoleon completed his bestselling book, *Think and Grow Rich*. Rosa Lee helped with this great book, typing and editing it. Additionally, with the help of his new wife,

Introduction

Napoleon discovered the principle of Cosmic Habit Force and published *How to Sell Your Way Through Life*. Unfortunately, the marriage didn't last long, and as a result, Napoleon lost everything of a material nature.

In 1941, while a recently divorced Napoleon was giving lectures in South Carolina, he met Annie Lou Norman, one of the attendees at his lectures. The couple started their courtship in 1941 and were married in 1943. One of the *Think and Grow Rich* copies in the Napoleon Hill Foundation office today was autographed by Napoleon in 1941 to Annie Lou as an "acquaintance," and then Napoleon signed it again in 1943 for her as his wife. Napoleon and Annie Lou would remain married until his death in 1970.

When Annie Lou died in 1984, she left a treasure of material to her nephew, Dr. Charlie Johnson. During his life, and when he passed away in 2019, this valuable collection was given to the Napoleon Hill Foundation. It was in this material that staff at the Foundation found the lectures in this book. Annie Lou had retained copies of these lectures, which were delivered while she and Napoleon were traveling around the country. In my opinion, these lectures cover some of the most important success principles, namely: Definiteness of Purpose, Going the Extra Mile, the Master Mind Alliance, Applied Faith, Self-Discipline, and Cosmic Habit Force. There is little doubt that the years spent with Annie Lou, lecturing and writing, were some of the most successful years of Napoleon's life.

Shortly after Annie Lou and Napoleon were married, they moved to California. Napoleon stayed very busy with several radio programs and speaking engagements. In 1945, Napoleon published *The Master-Key to Riches* book. Annie Lou was a tremendous help to my grandfather due to her business experience, as she had previously been an administrative assistant and bookkeeper for the president of Presbyterian College in Clinton, South Carolina.

In the 1950s, my grandfather published *How to Think Your Way to Wealth*, the title of which was later changed to *How to Raise Your Own Salary*. In 1952, while speaking at a dental convention in Chicago, he met W. Clement Stone. Mr. Stone challenged him to come out of retirement. These two men ended up working together for ten years and co-authored *Success Through a Positive Mental Attitude* in 1960. Together, they presented many seminars and lectures across the country, teaching the success principles that have positively impacted millions of people all over the world.

In the mid 1960s, Napoleon wrote a manuscript he titled *Success and Something Greater*. The publisher changed the title to *Grow Rich with Peace of Mind* when issuing the book in 1967. At this point in his life, Napoleon realized that true wealth was not in material possessions, but peace of mind. This was the last book he published before he died in 1970 at the age of 87.

My grandfather left a wealth of speeches, writings, and articles that were unpublished at the time of his death. Today, the nonprofit Napoleon Hill Foundation, started by Napoleon and Annie Lou in 1962, is proud to publish these works. A few years ago, for just one example, the Foundation published the never-before-seen manuscript titled *Outwitting the Devil*, written in 1938 and given to the Foundation by Dr. Johnson, which quickly became a bestselling book. My grandfather's lectures and speeches that were recorded on audio tapes contain a vast collection of valuable material for those seeking success in their lives. Three of his series of radio lectures were recently published in the "Napoleon Hill is on the Air" books, titled *Five Foundations for Success*, *Success Habits*, and *Adversity and Advantage*. The book before you is the result of yet more of this valuable material that helps keep his teachings and legacy alive all over the world. It consists of six lectures on major success principles, presented in 1947 with the support and help of Annie Lou. I hope you enjoy and benefit from it, as I have.

Preface

By Don M. Green

Millions have read, studied, and applied the principles of success that Napoleon Hill spent a lifetime developing. Fewer people know the part that the women in his life played in his success. These women are responsible in no small measure for his remarkable career.

James Monroe Hill, Napoleon Hill's father, finished his schooling at the age of 14 and went to work for his father. He cleared land, planted crops, and built a two-room cabin on Guest River, in rural Wise County, Virginia. By the time James was 20 years old, he was self-sufficient, and he was able to support a wife. He married Sarah Sylvania Blair and moved her into his log cabin. Very little is known about Sarah, who had two sons with James, Oliver Napoleon and Vivian. Sarah died when she was 24 years old. Napoleon was eight years old, and Vivian was six years old. The cause of Sarah's death at such a young age was referred to as "dropsy," which was an old term used frequently for death from unknown causes. Among the causes could have been heart failure.

Sarah had long been in ill health and was not in a good position to discipline the young Napoleon, who was prone to mischief and often in trouble. This was to change after his mother's death when his father married Martha Ramey Banner. Martha, the young widow of a high school principal and the daughter of a doctor, was a schoolteacher. She had three children of her own at the time of her marriage to James Hill: Warren, age six; Roy, age four; and Willie, age four. In 1895, she presented James with another son they named Paul.

This remarkable woman entered the lives of young Oliver Napoleon and his brother Vivian at a time when the boys desperately needed parental guidance. Napoleon reacted well to Martha's discipline, though, and later would remark about her in about the same manner that President Abraham Lincoln had said of his stepmother: "Anything I am or ever aspire to be I owe to that dear woman."

Martha was a strong-willed woman and took charge in the Hill household. She saw the need for drastic changes, and she welcomed the challenge. Martha displayed her willpower by insisting the entire family become regular and active members at the Powell River Primitive Baptist Church.

She was quick to form a relationship with her stepson Napoleon, who was a highly troubled and angry young boy. According to Hill's biography, Martha did not use stern discipline but instead built the young boy's confidence through encouragement. She said to her young stepson, "People are wrong about you, Napoleon. You are not the worst boy in Wise County, only the most active. You need to direct your energy toward accomplishing something worthwhile." During the conversation, Martha suggested that Napoleon become a writer because of his keen imagination and initiative. "If you will devote as much time to writing as you have to causing troubles," she concluded, "you might live to see the time when your influence will be felt throughout the state." This was the first time anyone other than his parents had given him words of encouragement. Under the watchful eye of the new woman in the household, Napoleon studied his books as never before. Martha provided the young boy much more help than was available in the lessons he obtained in school.

At the age of 12, Napoleon still possessed a six shooter. His stepmother proposed that he surrender his gun, saying she would replace it with a typewriter. In the rugged mountains of Southwest Virginia in the 1890s, a typewriter was indeed a rare (because expensive) item. Martha told her young stepson, "If you become as good with a typewriter as you are with that gun, you may become rich, famous, and well known throughout the world." With the encouragement of his stepmother, Napoleon began to understand how good writers could achieve fame far beyond local, state, and even national boundaries. Soon, he was seeing himself in the same universe as the great men whose books he was reading.

Napoleon and his brother Vivian eventually went to Georgetown University to study law. Martha's son Paul went on to attend medical school and become a surgeon in the United States Army. Paul served in World War II and was the attending physician when General George C. Patton was in a jeep accident near the end of the war. The Hill family legacy is a great example of how a strong-willed woman can make such a vast difference in promoting education and helping alleviate poverty, and the effects are still being felt over 100 years later.

Martha lived until 1941 and was able to see her time spent with her stepson prove worthwhile; she saw the young Napoleon get published in various newspapers and publish his own magazines. Martha was to see the publication of *The Law of Success* in 1928, which provided Napoleon with wealth and fame. The next book, *The Magic Ladder to Success*, was published in 1930. Napoleon published *Think and Grow Rich* in 1937, which became the best-selling self-help book of all time. Martha also saw the 1939 publication of *How to Sell Your Way Through Life*, which many consider a classic in the sales area.

It was at the end of 1908 that another woman came into Hill's life who would change it forever. It was a cold snowy December of that year when the 26-year-old Napoleon met Florence Elizabeth Horner, a pretty, young woman from Lumberport, West Virginia. They were both residents of Washington, DC, at the time. Florence was taking care of a young niece who had been stricken with polio. Though she was in her senior year in high school, Florence was already 20 years old, having delayed the start of school for several years, most likely due to family responsibilities. Florence was an excellent student who would soon graduate with honors. She spoke fluent German, possessed a thorough knowledge of chemistry, and had brilliant English skills.

Living in Washington, DC, Napoleon had become a man about town with good prospects for the future and marriage as well. Napoleon mixed well in social circles; he was handsome, personable, and exciting. He was seeking marriage only to the right woman from a good family. Napoleon did what he often did in the future: he resorted to advertising to accomplish his objective.

The ad was placed in *The Washington Times* Sunday edition, in the personal want ad section. It read, "Educated refined young businessman who just moved to Washington would like to meet refined young lady preferably not over 18 years old, object friendship and possibility of leading to matrimony; answers strictly confidential, and if desired, would meet any members of girl's family first and convince them of my good intentions and personal standing in my hometown. Address: Young Southerner, Box 27, Times Office." With the help of this ad, Napoleon met his future wife, Florence.

Florence did not answer the ad herself; it was her cousin, Ellen, who lived in the same house—a spacious and stately home. The meeting at such a magnificent residence must have been an eye-opening experience for someone born in a log cabin in the mountains of Southwest Virginia. Napoleon arrived at his appointment on time and rang to announce his presence, but it was not Ellen who answered the door. Ellen's cousin Florence was assigned the task.

Florence and Napoleon fell madly in love and courted under the watchful eye of her aunt, Myra. They planned to marry just after Florence's graduation from high school. However, the couple could not wait and eloped a few days prior to the planned wedding. They married on Thursday, July 20, 1910, in Marlboro, Virginia.

By every account, they made a lovely couple. Florence began the marriage as a homemaker and quickly became pregnant. Their first child, James Hornor Hill, was born on July 18, 1911. Shortly after Napoleon's marriage to Florence, he lost his investment in a motor car dealership. The National Automobile Supply Company failed, and he sought bankruptcy protection for it. Napoleon took refuge with Florence's affluent family in Lumberport, West Virginia.

Napoleon had a pattern of failed businesses throughout the 25 years he was married to Florence, and he continuously sought financial help from her well-to-do family. Once she even pawned her wedding ring. Over the course of their marraige, Florence quieted Napoleon's fears, sustained his ambitions, and gave him the sanctuary of a loving family with three sons. Their marriage ultimately ended after Florence lost hope in the restless and often absent man whom she had passionately loved for so many years.

After the divorce, Napoleon met Rosa Lee Beeland while on a speaking tour. Rosa Lee was the daughter of a railroad superintendent and had lived an affluent life, raised mostly by a maternal aunt. Rosa Lee's family was also southern gentry, abundant with lawyers and doctors. She was well educated for her time, intellectually curious, physically attractive, and about 20 years younger than Napoleon. In spite of their age difference, they had fallen in love, and after a year of courtship they married and settled in New York City, where Napoleon finished *Think and Grow Rich*, which was soon to become, and has remained, his best-selling book.

Napoleon's second son, Blair, lived with the newly married couple in New York City while *Think and Grow Rich* was being written. According to Blair, Napoleon walked around the small apartment dictating the book to Rosa Lee. They worked together on the book for about 20 hours a day for many weeks. When they were done, Rosa Lee edited the book and then typed several copies, which she mailed off to various publishers. Her help was crucial to the writing and publishing of *Think and Grow Rich*. The book immediately became a bestseller, and within five months it was printed three times. The number of copies increased each time: 5,000 on the first printing, 10,000 on the second, and 20,000 on the third. Over a million copies were sold before the Great Depression was over, and 50 years later more than 20 million copies had been sold.

Rosa Lee also contributed to the 1939 publication of *How to Sell Your Way Through Life*.

They were then living in Mount Dora, Florida, in a castle, and Hill was driving a Rolls Royce automobile, both made possible by *Think and Grow Rich*. In spite of their success, the age difference was too great, and their marriage soon failed.

Shortly before World War II started, Rosa Lee joined the Women's Auxiliary Corps and learned to fly. Later, Rosa Lee served with General MacArthur during the occupation of Japan. After the end of World War II, Rosa Lee moved to New York City and worked as an associate editor of *Popular Mechanics Magazine*. In 1962, when President John F. Kennedy was establishing the Peace Corps as a means of helping other countries, Rosa Lee joined it and served in Micronesia. She was clearly a woman of substance, and her contributions to Napoleon Hill's success were very significant. Their divorce became final on March 5, 1941. Napoleon remarked that he lost everything except his typewriter in the divorce, but he also reflected that his time with Rosa Lee was worth it.

Before the year was out, Napoleon Hill was drawn to the little town of Clinton, South Carolina, by William Plummer Jacobs, who was president of Presbyterian College, the owner of Jacobs Press, and a public relations counselor to a group of South Carolina textile firms. Jacobs was a follower of Hill's work and asked him to rewrite the entire philosophy of personal achievement as a self-help course of instruction and to create a lecture series called "The Philosophy of American Achievement" that would be tested and perfected at Presbyterian College, then delivered to schools, towns, and factories throughout South Carolina. Napoleon accepted the invitation and took an apartment on the third floor of a large building in Clinton. With all his failures behind him, Napoleon took on a new vision, closing the door on his past life as a "millionaire author" who had let success go to his head. He was enthusiastic about his new opportunity in Clinton.

After settling in Clinton, Napoleon concentrated on his work and kept mostly to himself. Although he did not know it at the time, he had caught the attention of Jacobs's secretary, Annie Lou Norman. Annie Lou was 47 years old and had never married. She had dated various gentlemen but had never met a man for whom she had a desire. Annie Lou had the charm and grace of a southern belle. She was said to have the soul of a social worker but the business sense of a comptroller. Intelligent beyond her years, Annie Lou grew her responsibilities and influence at a fast pace. When Jacobs took over for his father, Annie Lou knew the business inside and out. She kept the account ledger, corresponded with authors, edited manuscripts, and evaluated submissions.

When Napoleon Hill showed up in 1941 in Clinton, Annie Lou was thoroughly aware of his literary accomplishments. She and her sister Lela took one of his classes at Presbyterian College. The lectures were interesting to Annie Lou on an intellectual level, but because she had already mastered the steps to financial wellness, she did not need to adopt the principles Napoleon discussed to achieve financial success. Instead, she became to be more and more fascinated with Napoleon himself.

By the fall of 1941, Napoleon and Annie Lou were openly interested in each other. Theirs was no whirlwind romance. Annie Lou was cautiously looking for something better than what she already possessed. Napoleon was busy teaching and lecturing in Clinton and working with LeTourneau Company of Georgia and its 2,000 employees. He spent most weekends in Clinton, where his courtship of Annie Lou would not be hurried; and for once in his life, he enjoyed the slower pace.

They were a study in opposites. Hill was outwardly a crowd-pleasing man with a flair for showmanship, and Annie Lou was a private woman given to moderation. Hill created; Annie Lou conserved. Napoleon tended to be spontaneous; Annie Lou was deliberate. Annie Lou and Napoleon became friends first, then very close friends, then intimates. This was the way chosen by Annie Lou. She was familiar with the mess that the Rosa Lee marriage had caused and was in no hurry. Their relationship involved her close family and a large number of friends as well. This was true especially with her sister Lela and Lela's son Charles. Annie Lou and Napoleon married in late 1943 after a lengthy courtship.

Preface

In 1941, Napoleon gave Annie Lou an autographed, first-edition, hardcover copy of *Think and Grow Rich*. The book was signed and dated again with the following notation: "You had the book and now you have the author. December 23, 1943, Napoleon Hill." This is the only Napoleon Hill book known in existence that was signed by him twice. The 1943 date was the day before their wedding took place. (Today, the book is proudly displayed in the archives at the Napoleon Hill Foundation, located on the campus of the University of Virginia's College at Wise.) Annie Lou brought a great change in Napoleon's outlook. Just two years before, during Christmas, he was in isolation, a broken soul, facing financial ruin and personally humiliated. Now he had a strong-willed, loving wife and friendships in Clinton with some of the very best people he would ever know.

Annie Lou and Napoleon left on their honeymoon, then visited friends and Annie Lou's relatives, and then left for California. They had found each other and built a foundation for a long, loving marriage. Before leaving for California, Annie Lou made sure Napoleon had a plan and was not just wandering from one location to another. She displayed her strong will and business savvy, which kept them on solid financial footings that lasted for the 27 years of their marriage and the 14 years she lived as a widow. Her will showed that she still was very financially secure at the time of her death. Her business sense and Hill's creative skills were an excellent combination that produced success.

Napoleon was 59 years old when the newlyweds arrived in California. The reason he wanted to settle in California was to seek new territory to work. California was the perfect place for them. It had a booming economy with a growing population. Hill had made few appearances in California, but he was already popular there through his books. It was said the County of Los Angeles Library had 70 copies of *Think and Grow Rich* on its bookshelves. Napoleon told Annie Lou he could fill lecture halls in California for years, and he was right.

In California, Annie Lou and Napoleon had a steady income and enjoyed life together. Napoleon had numerous radio programs that were very popular. He continued to work on his lifelong crusade of teaching the principles of personal achievement. During this time, Annie Lou not only managed the household, but she also managed Napoleon's business. During the three years that the Los Angeles radio show aired, Hill also traveled, spoke, and wrote at a breakneck speed.

Annie Lou helped Napoleon stay focused with her pragmatic and iron-willed concentration on things that mattered. She was good at curtailing his tendency to pursue too many projects at the same time. Annie Lou also steered him away from the con men and charlatans who had always found in the guileless Napoleon an easy mark. What Annie Lou gave to Napoleon was much more important than business help. She gave him a family life that he had never known, or accepted, in all his adult life.

Preface

Annie Lou traveled with Napoleon on many of his trips when he was fulfilling lecturing obligations. She corresponded with Napoleon's three sons with Florence—David, Blair, and James. Although a full reconciliation with Napoleon and his sons never happened, Annie Lou's efforts did help Napoleon overcome some guilt over his earlier failings as a father.

In Annie Lou's personal collection left at her death in 1984, a wealth of material was preserved, including six lectures from the summer of 1947 that are reproduced in this book. Also found in the personal files were checks dated in July 1947 signed by Annie Lou. One $50 check is made out to stenographer Betty Wallace, dated July 8, 1947, for the transcription of seven lectures Hill performed (the seventh lecture has not been found). Another check dated July 8, 1947, for $460, is made out to The Friday Morning Club and signed by Annie Lou Hill, for the rental of a lecture hall.

Her files shed no more light on the circumstances surrounding these lectures. This never-before-published material is being furnished to promote the work that Napoleon Hill did in his long career, writing, speaking, and conducting classes on the principles of success. As with so much of his earlier work, it was prepared and presented with the assistance of the important woman in his life at that time. I hope that this preface and J.B. Hill's introduction provide a sense of the hugely important roles that Napoleon's stepmother and wives played in the development and teaching of his success principles.

CHAPTER ONE

Definiteness of Purpose

May 14, 1947

Definiteness of purpose is the starting point of all achievement. It is also the stumbling block of 98 out of 100 people, because they never really and truly get started with anything approaching definiteness of purpose.

You may be surprised when I tell you that out of over 35,000 people whom I have taught and analyzed personally, only two out of every hundred had anything even akin to definiteness of purpose, and those two are the ones who are succeeding. They are the Henry Fords, the Henry J. Kaisers, the Frank Vanderlips, and they are the people who are not settling with life for anything short of what they want. I hope every one of you will resolve that from here on out, you will not settle with life for anything less than what you want. Will you do that? I hope I shall convince you before we are through working together that you don't have to settle for anything less than what you want. I am not just using idle words; I am saying that based on observation of thousands of people. I have found so many times that if a man really and truly wants to get a thing, he can do it. If you don't have the ambition to start making life pay off on your own terms, there isn't anything I can do, unless I can break you down and make you have a definiteness of purpose. I might be able to do that, too, to make you into a changed person.

With your help, I can.

> I hope that every one of you will resolve that from here on out, you will not settle with life for anything less than what you want.

There are certain factors that enter into this subject of definiteness of purpose that are classified as mental, certain factors that might be classified as spiritual, and certain factors that might be classified as economic. I am going to talk about all of them. I am going to break down each one of the subjects and build them up into a solid whole and explain all of their connections with the subject of definiteness of purpose.

Before I begin breaking them down, I want to tell you something that happened to me in 1919 that will give you a very fine example of what I mean. I don't know of a better way I can illustrate this principle than by what I am now going to tell you.

When World War I ended, I went into my bank vault, took out my definite chief aim I had written out, turned to

Definiteness of Purpose

the paragraph that I had written for 1919, and read, "I will earn $10,000 in 1919." I ran my fountain pen through the "$10,000" and wrote over it "$100,000" because I had determined to publish and edit the *Golden Rule Magazine*, and I knew that I would need at least $100,000. Previously, I had been getting along nicely on $10,000 operating a school, and it was all I needed at the time, but I knew a magazine would require much more capital.

I laid this document back in the bank vault, and just a little while after that a man came up from Texas. He came into my office and introduced himself. He took me to lunch, stayed around there three or four days, and finally said, "I came all the way from Texas to see you. I want to take you to the Texas oil fields and show you what happens to the men who get rich overnight. They are all trying to get something for nothing. If you will come down, I will gladly pay all your expenses." I was tickled to death to accept the opportunity. I went all through the oil fields with him and had a grand time. He took me down to the railroad station to see me off. As I was preparing to go into the coach, he shook hands with me and said, "Mr. Hill, I would like you to come back to Texas and spend three weeks out of each month working with me, and at the end of the year I will pay you $100,000 if you will stay with me the entire year." At that time the signal had been given and the train was starting to move. I called back and asked him when he wanted me to be here, and he said, "As soon as you can make it."

I went down there and spent four months. He drew up a contract that said if I quit short of a year, I wouldn't get the $100,000. Within one month I had performed so well that I had earned the $100,000, and soon after that he made it so difficult for me that I had to resign, which was part of his original plan, no doubt. I went back to Chicago and didn't get a nickel of my money.

At this point, there may be students in my class who don't know why I didn't get my money and some who do. I want you to remember this. Suppose I had added the two words to that sentence I had written about my definite major purpose. "I will earn *and receive* $100,000 during the year of 1919." Do you think that would have made any difference? Yes, I think you get the point.

Just what difference would it have made if I had added those two words? Would he have paid me? I'll tell you. I would have written it into my consciousness and into my contract; and I would have taken it into my lawyer, and he would have seen that the man paid me. That's the difference it would have made.

In writing out a definite major purpose, I want you to know it is something like taking a picture. If you have ever had an experience with a camera, you will know that there are three things that enter into taking a good picture. First, you have to get it properly focused. Second, timing is important, and third (and maybe this should be first) is the light. You must observe those three things, otherwise you will not get a clear, satisfactory picture. You will get a blurred picture, or maybe no picture at all. The subconscious mind is like the sensitive plate of a camera, and when you put on that plate a wishy-washy, indefinite picture of what you want, you may be sure you will get a blurred result.

There isn't anyone in this room who doesn't have hopes or wishes. What I am talking about tonight has nothing to do with hopes or wishes. It has to do with your putting on the plate such a clear picture of what you want that you can't fail to convey to your subconscious mind precisely what you want, when you want it, and what you are going to give in return for it.

The subconscious mind—a lot of writers and philosophers, including myself, have a lot to say about it, and not any of us knows very much about it. We do know you have some source inside of you that very clearly resembles the plate of a camera and you can transfer a picture onto this sensitized plate. And if you can make it clear and the timing is right—the timing is very important—something inside of you takes hold of that picture and begins to move forward, using every available means to carry it out and transfer it into its physical equivalent. We know that it works that way.

> *The subconscious mind is like the sensitive plate of a camera, and when you put on that plate a wishy-washy, indefinite picture of what you want, you may be sure you will get a blurred result.*

One of the most astounding experiences I had in preparing this philosophy was to observe that the successful men I interviewed put their subconscious minds to work and they harvested the better part of their minds' efforts while they slept. R. G. LeTourneau, with whom I was associated for a year and a half, is a very outstanding example of what I mean. Without special experience, capital, or very much of anything, he had astounding success with this principle that I am talking about tonight. Mr. LeTourneau's greatest asset consisted in the fact that he could transfer to his subconscious mind what he wanted to do while he was asleep, and his subconscious mind then gets busy and does it. He says he is associated with God when he does this. I have my own notions, and I suppose you have, too. I am not going to question whom he is in partnership with. What interested me was that he manipulates his own mind and makes life pay off on his own terms. If Mr. LeTourneau could do it, you and I can do it.

I want you to recognize tonight that there is a power within you, and you don't have to ask anybody for the privilege of using this power—a power so great that you can get anything you want in life. I won't qualify that either. I used to say, "within reason." Now I say, "Whatever you want in life you are capable of producing."

Someone may say, "Suppose I had been born with a physical disability?" You would think you had me there, wouldn't you? Oh, no, you wouldn't have me there at all! Some of the grandest people I have known, some of the most successful people, have been physically handicapped and have had useful, successful lives. Charles Steinmetz was like that, and the world has never known a greater genius in his field. My son Blair is like that. Blair was born without ears, and he runs rings around many other boys in everything he does in life, especially in relating himself to other people.

If you have something you don't like, just remember that if you are going to hang onto something you don't want, or let it hang onto you, you can at least change your mental attitude so that that person or thing does not irritate you. You can do that. I know that because I have done it. When you get onto this principle of definiteness of purpose—really and truly know how to apply it—on the one hand you will make it throw off the things you don't want, and on the other hand it gives you the things you do want. Isn't that a marvelous tool to have around?

The reason I said in the beginning of this lecture that you would go out of here a changed person is just that. The carcass may be the same, but the things inside of it will be a different person. And you are going to start tonight in settling with life for nothing short of what you want. If you do, you and I will get along splendidly, and you will see marvelous results—results as near to a miracle as anything you will ever know.

My big trouble in getting started with students is that they think I must have some ulterior motive, and so far as I am concerned, I have no ulterior motive except to introduce to you the benefits of life and the source by which you make those benefits permanent. I have nothing to sell you, nothing to gain. I am free now to pass on to you the knowledge that will really and truly give you freedom of body and mind in the future. I want you to know that. I want you to recognize it. I hope that you will know that I am far too intelligent to make that statement before a group of intelligent people if I couldn't back it up.

My greatest difficulty in dealing with people is to shake them loose from the past. If I can succeed in shaking you loose from your past, you may be sure that your future will be something you want—something different and better than you had in the past. I may not be able to shake you loose entirely tonight, but somewhere along the line I will shake you loose. You may be sure of that.

Some people today say success is available only to the genius and have assumed that there are certain types of people in this world you could properly call geniuses only because they are born that way. I found out in the last 38 years what are the ingredients which make up geniuses. Shall I give them to you?

Here are the ingredients, my friends, that go into geniuses. It is not something I read out of books, but it is out of the lives of outstanding men of this nation where I got my philosophy.

The first thing that goes into geniuses is Definiteness of Purpose. I never heard of a genius in my life who didn't know what he wanted to do in life. They all know and are busy doing it.

The second factor is Applied Faith—not just a belief in faith, but applied faith. And you couldn't make application of this rule unless you had definiteness of purpose. Definiteness of purpose is the foundation upon which all faith is based.

> *Definiteness of purpose is the foundation upon which all faith is based.*

The third factor is something I want you to catch, and that is Enthusiasm. If you can catch as much as I have to throw off, you will really catch fire. There would be no object in having definiteness of purpose if you didn't have some fire under you. Enthusiasm causes you to have fire.

And the fourth factor is Imagination.

The fifth factor is Motive, and in just a few moments, I will give you the nine basic motives of life. And incidentally, nobody does anything without a motive. It may be a hidden motive or a subconscious motive, but there has to be a motive back of everything.

The sixth factor is Personal Initiative backed by intense action. You will never be a genius unless you get into the habit of doing things without somebody telling you.

The seventh factor is Going the Extra Mile. You will never be a genius unless you make it your business all through life to engage in extracurricular services of some sort every day of your life.

And the eighth factor is a Master Mind alliance with other people. How many? That depends on what you want to accomplish in life. I had a Master Mind alliance in building this philosophy of over 500 top men in this country. I had the privilege of going to school by talking to them, learning from them, taking advantage of their trial and error. And without that cooperation, I would have had to have 100 lives to develop the philosophy. I couldn't have done it by myself. Your object in life being different, you may not require more than a dozen—maybe a half dozen lives, maybe one. But if you are going to be a genius, you will have to learn to take advantage of other people's brains, and I hope you will take advantage of my brain. Don't be afraid to ask. Don't be timid.

The ninth factor is perhaps the most important of all—a Positive Mental Attitude. You certainly never will rank as a genius until you learn to positivize your mind and keep it that way at will.

Those are the factors that go into genius. Many of those factors you already have. You will be able to take inventory of yourself before this course is over and learn which are missing, and we have a means of supplying you with the missing ones, whatever they may be.

Definiteness of Purpose

We come now to the starting point of the seven fundamental premises essential to attaining personal achievement, and I will break them down so that you will understand what these component parts are.

The first, which is the starting point of all individual achievement, is the adoption of a definite purpose, accompanied by a definite plan, and followed by appropriate action. That is the beginning of all achievement. Whether your purpose is great or small, you must go through that. Wishing for it, hoping for it—yes, even praying for it—is not going to assure you getting it. There is something more definite. And if you go through this routine, then when you get down to prayer, I will guarantee the prayer will be answered much more quickly and more to your liking after you have done your part.

> *The starting point of all individual achievement is the adoption of a definite purpose, accompanied by a definite plan, and followed by appropriate action.*

Second, all individual achievement is the result of a motive or combination of motives. The nine basic motives are the ABCs of success. And unless you are familiar with these, you will not learn to excel. You must have them. They are the fundamentals that you must deal with. For instance, in choosing your major purpose in life, if you don't place back of your purpose a proper number of these motives, you are not going to be invested in carrying out that major purpose after you adopt it. A burning desire goes to the subconscious mind to initiate action. A burning desire behind your definite purpose is necessary, and you are not going to have a burning desire unless you have a motive that literally sets you on fire. And the more of those motives that you have urging you on, the more likely you are to get in touch with the subconscious mind.

Number one, the greatest of all motives—love. And when we speak of love, we have reference not merely to physical attraction; we have reference to love in its broader sense. There are many things in which we should express love every day. We should make our daily prayers, prayers of gratitude, not for the things we want, but for what we already have. And as you learn to pray this way, you will find that you attract more of those things to you.

The second of the nine basic motives is the motive of sex. Nature is a very ingenious planner, and I get my basis for this from Nature. Nature has created this marvelous motive of sex as a means of perpetuating every species on earth, even the things that grow out of the ground. The vegetation—even the electrons and protons of matter—are based upon the principle of sex. If you combine the emotions of sex and love and put them behind men and women, you will see that an enormous power comes out of that.

Motive number three is the desire for material wealth or money. You combine those three—the emotion of love, the emotion of sex, and the desire for material wealth—and you won't be watching the clock. You will be much more anxious to get through the job than you are to get away from it. And you won't feel that work is a burden; you will feel it is a privilege—a blessed privilege—because you will be driven by these three basic motives.

The fourth is the desire for self-preservation. Everybody is motivated by that. I won't need to go into that very much.

The fifth is the desire for freedom of body and mind. And incidentally, you will notice that these motives are very definitely related—the desire for freedom of mind and body and wealth. There are a great many people who want wealth so that they can have freedom of body and mind. That's the only thing I can think of that I want money for. Otherwise, I can go out and sleep in the great outdoors in a pup tent.

The next is the desire for self-expression. I am working much harder for the freedom to express myself and gain public recognition than for any amount of money, and there are a great many people who are just like that. And if you don't know that, you will not be able to gain full cooperation from people, even though you have a Master Mind alliance.

The next is the desire for life after death. It is a very strong motive, and on that motive all religious activity is based.

Now here come the only two negative motives in the whole lot, and they are important because they are very powerful.

Number eight is the desire for revenge. You will be astounded to know how much ingenuity some people put into the desire for revenge—the desire to strike back. "I'll take it out of his pocket or hang his hide on the barn door." How often have you heard that or its equivalent? It's a motive for action, and a very strong one, but a desire that will kick back on anybody who has it—you may be sure of that.

Number nine is the emotion of fear. Fear is one of the most outstanding of all the motives and keeps you in poverty all through life. Often it keeps you from using your personal initiative, and under this heading are the seven basic fears, all of which should be conquered if you are going to eliminate this negative. Here they are:

The fear of poverty. Until you get that fear out of your consciousness, you are not going to get ahead in this philosophy until you start living and feeling just as if you had all the money you need. I had a student who wanted a million dollars. He wrote himself a check and slipped it under his pillow every night. He never did get the million dollars, or hadn't the last time I communicated with him, and I found out why. He said he put it under his pillow and said, "I don't suppose it will work out, but I hope it will." In other words, he had his fingers crossed when he set his definite purpose of a million dollars. You must not do any finger crossing.

The next fear is the fear of criticism. My, oh my, what this does to people! The fear of criticism stymies a lot of people—keeps them from exploiting ideas that would give them independence if they would only act on their own initiative. Salesmen will tell you that 75 percent of the people whom they approach, if it happens to be a man, he will say, "I'll think it over and talk it over with my wife." He doesn't intend to talk it over with his wife. He just wants to avoid making a decision.

The fear of the loss of love is the fear upon which that form of dementia praecox called jealousy is based. If you don't think fear of the loss of love causes a lot of trouble, you haven't been around divorce courts very much. Love is one of the greatest things in the world, but not worth sacrificing a life over.

And the next fear—and I am talking about all the things you are going to get rid of by definiteness of purpose, and I will get around to that in a little while—the fourth is the fear of ill health. I made a survey a few years ago among doctors in all fields of therapy by which it was shown that 75 percent of the people who go to doctors' offices are suffering with nothing more serious than hypochondria, a five-dollar word that means "imaginary illness." I am not talking about the people who are bedridden. You can make yourself sick and make yourself well by the way you use your mind. There are often things you have to have a surgeon's knife for, and there are times when you have to have a dentist's forceps and have your teeth taken out. Your mind won't do away with bad teeth. I happen to know.

The fifth of these seven basic fears is the fear of the loss of liberty, and that shows up in connection with people's jobs where they are working for wages and salaries. It shows up in a great many different ways. It showed up in international affairs a few years back, and we just missed losing our liberty. And unless we start protecting what we have, we shall see the day when we lose our liberty in this country.

The sixth of these seven basic fears is one I like to jump on with both feet. It's the fear of old age. I discovered when I had a birthday, the proper thing was to take a year off my age instead of adding one. I really and truly began to change appearance and to feel young simply because I sold myself to the idea of youth instead of old age.

I made a survey of the outstanding men of the world back down through the ages, and I discovered that the men of greatest achievement in life started their best work after age 55, and some did their best work after 60 and 70. The reason for that is that with age, Nature compensates you for the loss of youth with one of the greatest things in the world. I wonder if you could tell me what that is? Wisdom—experience, you sometimes call it.

I had a mighty good time when I was 20, 25, and 30, but I wouldn't want to go back to that age again. I wasn't as useful to the world as I am now. I couldn't earn a living as easy as I do it now. I could stay up longer hours and get around at night better than I do now, but I don't want to stay up nights now. Of course, with age you lose your teeth, but after all, the dentists can supply you nowadays with a set far better than your own.

The wig man can do the same thing with hair and give you any color you want.

The seventh and last of these seven basic fears is the grandfather of them all. I have always been at a loss to describe to my students how to whip this. It's a humdinger. It's a universal one. What I can do is to tell you how I defeated it. This is the fear of death. I whipped the fear of death by analyzing what we call life and what we call death. And by observing the way Nature works, I could see that there are only a few things in the entire universe that we can recognize and isolate, and those are time, space, energy, matter, and the thing back of all those—intelligence. Those five things are all Nature has to work with, and I learned in elementary physics that you can neither create nor destroy energy or matter. You can transfer it from one thing to another, but you cannot destroy it. Consequently, if you can't create or destroy energy or matter, you can't destroy life, and Nature doesn't destroy it either. And that which we call life probably goes back to the universal well so that the next fellow who gets it probably has a little better to work with than we had.

Then finally, I said, "Life is probably one of two things: either that which we call death is just one long eternal sleep"—and I don't know of very many things in this world I enjoy more than sleep—"or else, if it isn't sleep, it's an experience on some other plane far better than we have on this earth. And in either event, there is nothing to fear, because it's going to come anyway."

When we get around to reasoning like that, you take this fear of death and write it off. You don't discuss it or think about it. I can truthfully tell you I am not any more concerned over death than I am over what I am going to eat tomorrow. I will go at one time or another, and there is nothing I can do about it. And I certainly would be a simple-minded person if I devoted any of my time to worrying about it.

Anything you fear will trail you around like a pet dog—including poverty, including ill health, including the fear of criticism. If you fear criticism, you may be sure you will get it. The mind attracts to it the counterpart of that which it dwells upon.

You may be interested to learn that the majority of people go all the way through life fixing the mind on what they don't want —and getting every bit of it. Wouldn't it be a good idea to refuse to think about the things you don't want, feed your mind with the things you do want, until you start getting them? That is one of the greatest things that you could do with definiteness of purpose. I don't know anything in your entire life more important to you than to learn the art of doing that, because when your mind has definiteness of purpose, you are then in a condition to start having faith. And when you have faith, you can call upon that great store of Infinite Intelligence to carry out your wishes.

The mind attracts to it the counterpart of what which it dwells upon.

Definiteness of Purpose

Have you ever thought of the reason why prayer generally doesn't work? Has it ever occurred to you that there is something wrong with the way you pray? I can tell you that prayer always works, but not the way you want it. When you go to prayer with your fingers crossed after everything else has failed, and you only half believe you will get it, then usually you don't. The dominating portion of your thought—your desire—is negative, and you may be sure that Infinite Intelligence will give you a negative answer.

I can truthfully tell you that never in my life did I start out to do anything or achieve anything that I didn't get if I conditioned my mind properly before I started it. It all depends on the way you condition your mind. If I were selling life insurance and somebody gave me a rate book, if I were not eager to get in to see a man, if I were the slightest bit afraid, I would not go in until I conditioned my mind and would be glad to talk to him. You will never sell anybody unless you sell the thing first to yourself. He might buy something from you, but you wouldn't sell it to him.

Definiteness of purpose will enable you to condition your mind to get anybody to do anything you want him to do, but be very careful that you don't ask anybody to do anything not beneficial to himself. Nature not only compensates you, but she penalizes you for that which you took away from other people. The reason I emphasize that in such strong terms is that I want to remember that myself, and there are a lot of people you know who ought to remember that. Don't you think?

Consider how a lot of people deal with others. They always want to get in the back door and come out with something they are not entitled to. Go the second mile? They don't even go the first mile. They are looking for something without giving proper return for it. Isn't that the condition of the majority of people in the world today? I don't want it to be that way with you. I have a better way of teaching you how to get the things you want, and everybody will be glad to let you have them.

There is one thing about Mr. Henry Ford that I have always admired—giving millions of people work—and that definite major purpose was a benefit to all. That is the only way to have a definite purpose at any time—so that the purpose will benefit everybody whom it affects.

We come now to the third premise of individual achievement, and it is this: any dominating idea, plan, or purpose held in the mind through repetition of thought and emotionalized with a burning desire for its realization is taken over by the subconscious section of the mind and acted upon almost instantaneously through whatever natural and logical means that may be available. That burning desire is all important. It is the condition of your mind that causes voluntary action in the subconscious mind. The subconscious mind is operating all the time.

> *Any dominating idea, plan, or purpose held in the mind through repetition of thought and emotionalized with a burning desire for its realization is taken over by the subconscious section of the mind and acted upon almost instantaneously through whatever natural and logical means that may be available.*

The fourth premise is that any dominating desire, plan, or purpose which is backed by that state of mind known as faith is taken over by the subconscious section of the mind and acted upon immediately.

The fifth premise is the power of thought—the only thing over which the human being has complete control, a fact so astounding that it signifies a close connection between the mind of man and Infinite Intelligence. I think there is no fact in connection with this philosophy that is more astounding than this fact—that you have control over one thing and one thing only—not your wife or your husband or your relatives, but there is one thing you have been given complete control over. Your body can be in prison, but your mind cannot. Now, the meaning I get out of that is that the Creator must have thought that was the most important thing in the world, because that is the only thing you have been given the right of control over. You can make your mind positive and attract the things you want, or you can make it negative and attract the things you don't want.

The mind is like a garden spot. You can reap a fine crop of weeds in the garden. Nature goes to work and plants all the things you don't want. But you can plant seeds, and Nature will be just as abundant in producing the things you do want. It is the same with the human mind. You can plant anything which you choose, and if you don't plant things that are beneficial to you, you may be sure these other seeds will take the mind over and you will not be in possession of it at any time. Definiteness of purpose will keep your mind clear of the things you don't want and keep it so busy working on the things you do want it has no time to gather weeds.

The sixth premise is Infinite Intelligence. The subconscious section of the mind appears to be the only doorway to Infinite Intelligence. This doorway is opened through faith based upon definiteness of purpose. I don't know of any other way of approaching the great storehouse of Infinite Intelligence except by faith expressed behind definiteness of purpose.

The seventh premise: Every brain is both a broadcasting station and a receiving station for the vibrations of thought, a fact which explains the importance of moving with definiteness of purpose instead of drifting, since the brain may be so thoroughly inspired with definiteness of purpose that it will begin to attract the physical appearance of that purpose. We had radio before Lee de Forest discovered the radio tube. We all carry around a radio in the brain, picking up vibrations and oftentimes acting upon them and imagining that they originated with ourselves.

The only time I am bothered with vibrations I don't want is when I am getting up in the morning. When I wake up and put my feet out of bed, somebody will say, "I guess it doesn't look so good; it looks foggy out there." Or maybe, "I don't feel so good today," or "Things aren't going to go so good today," and I immediately say something. I tell my mind, "I don't want any of those tramps in there," and then in a little while, my mind is so filled with the things I am going to do today I have no place for worry or fear or to make any limitations. In other words, my mind is hitting on all 12 cylinders. It is on the beam. Unless you remember to keep your mind on the beam you will not get anywhere. You will not be prosperous.

Now I am going to give you the essential principle of applying definiteness of purpose. First, write out a clear statement of your major purpose, sign it, commit it to memory, and repeat it at least once a day in the form of a prayer or affirmation. You don't have to be a religious person, or belong to any church, or make any religious proclamations whatsoever in order to carry out the suggestions I am giving you, but those of you who do have faith in prayer will see what a great advantage it gives you if you make your definite major purpose the subject of prayer.

The writing out of your definite major purpose is important; and when I speak of a major purpose, I want you to form a habit of acting with definiteness of purpose. Everything you do should be done with definiteness of purpose. Don't do anything in a wishy-washy way, but definitely. Everything you do, get into the habit of training your mind to be very specific about everything you want. It will be a little difficult at first, but when you get on to it, you will find that discipline becomes the master.

There are a lot of people who say, "I know what I want. What's the use of writing it out." There's a big difference between just planting an idea in your mind and going to the trouble of putting it on paper, because putting it on paper is the first step in the business of translating your impulse into a reality. And in the process of writing out your description, you will find you clarify your idea and get a transference into your subconscious mind in just the way you want it. If it isn't just the way to suit you, you can edit it, change it, or modify it. Don't neglect this important part of writing out the things you want to do. And if you are not ready yet to write out your major purpose, your overall purpose, the things you want to have for a lifetime, start writing out your major purpose for today or tomorrow, how you are going to do it, and what you are going to do, and you will be surprised how much more quickly you can accomplish things when you are specific and definite about it.

If you have a friend, and he says, "I'm glad to see you. Come over and see me sometime," what would you infer that he meant? You would infer that he was telling a lie and just trying to be nice. If he really meant it, he would say, "Listen, old friend, the wife and I would like to have you over to dinner tomorrow night at 6:30. Will you be there?" You would know that he really wanted you there. Be sure you remember the story I told tonight about the $100,000. Be sure you are as specific as you would be about writing a contract with a man that you wanted to do business with.

Next, write out a clear, definite outline of the plan or plans by which you intend to achieve the object of your purpose, and state the maximum of time in which you intend to attain it. Then describe precisely what you intend to give for it. Don't start out to get something for nothing.

If you will stick to those instructions, you will very likely attain your overall purpose and your minor purpose. Keep this within the range of what can be expected of a man or woman with your capabilities, age, and intelligence, but let me caution you not to be afraid to think big—think in big terms for yourself. Don't be afraid. If you have a dominating thought, it is probably not in the nature of overrating yourself but probably in the nature of underrating yourself and selling yourself short.

Keep your major purpose in life strictly to yourself except insofar as you will receive further instructions in the lesson on the Master Mind. You can get along with your enemies because you are watching them, but your friends are often very dangerous. They will get a wallop, a belly blow, under you before you know it. Keep it to yourself and only speak of it with deeds, not with words. Let the thing speak for itself. Actions are what count. There are people in this world who have nothing to do except to stand on the sidelines of life and stick out their foot just to see you tumble down. And if they find out your purpose, they will be lying in wait for you. But if you don't tell them which way you are going, they won't be there, or have an opportunity to discourage you, or put obstacles in your way, or cause other people to put obstacles in your way. They won't have that chance.

> **Speak of your definite major purpose only with deeds, not with words.**

It is surprising how people will tell everybody their business on a train. They will tell strangers everything. Learn to keep things to yourself—the things that are your own. Don't give away your trade secrets. When I speak of trade secrets, I am referencing the things that will get you where you want to be in life—and you won't be bothered with busybodies who are not going anywhere themselves and don't want anybody else to go. That's the reason for keeping your definite major purpose to yourself except insofar as you will have to disclose it to your Master Mind allies. But remember, when you get around to that Master Mind alliance, that will be with people who have proven their right to your confidence, and they are an integral part of your mind. In order to get the full benefit of their mind and education and experience, you will have to keep no secrets between you.

Our greatest demonstration of the useful application of the Definiteness of Purpose principle may be seen in how Nature applies this in the orderliness of the universe and the interrelation of all natural laws. Isn't it a marvelous thing to know that they are all coordinated? No man, no power known to man, can interfere with Nature's progress, whatever it happens to be. She relates the purpose of the stars, the solar system, the timing of the seasons, the forcing of water downhill, the growing of things, the producing of an oak tree from an acorn. Nature never makes a mistake, and she grows a pine tree from an acorn. Everything is so definite because everything is run by a system of laws, all coordinated. Wouldn't it be marvelous if individuals could order their lives as definitely as Nature orders things?

You can see what would happen if Nature didn't have that definiteness of purpose. There would be chaos. The planets wouldn't stay on their courses. There has to be definiteness of purpose in connection with Nature, and there has to be definiteness of purpose with the individual. He would be a goldfish in a bowl unless he has his whole life ordered, laid out, and controlled, by definiteness of purpose.

I know if I took the parts of my watch and shook them in my hat, they wouldn't reassemble themselves. There had to be a plan back of the making of that watch, and there has to be a plan back of the universe, and there has to be a plan back of the individual himself—and the individual himself controls that plan. He shouldn't leave it to chance or turn it over to anybody else.

"God moves in mysterious ways his wonders to perform." And when a great catastrophe takes place, it may be true that what seems to be evil is the greater good, and Nature is carrying out her plans in order that she can build and build better. She works in that way. She is constantly tearing down or building up and reassembling. Man is not in the same condition he came into this world. We are undergoing constant changes in the shape of our bodies and everything else. Everything in the universe is constantly undergoing changes, and in the change of human nature lies the possibility of improvement. Wouldn't it be sad if none of us could change? Don't you know a lot of people who need changing? Nature has fixed it so that we can improve no matter how many evils may overtake us. We may change them by changing our method of thinking, by changing our habits—especially our habits of paralyzed thinking.

In the change of human nature lies the possibility of improvement.

Somewhere along the line—it may not be the first or the second lesson—but I am going to break up your established habits that haven't been helping you. I had a student down in Georgia, and he acted so differently after he started my course that the president of the bank where he worked had him shadowed and finally found out he was going to my classes, and the detective enrolled in my class and became one of the best students. What made the president so sure something was wrong was that this man had such a fixed personality he couldn't make friends, and all of a sudden everybody who came into the bank asked for him, and that made the president suspicious. I broke up his bad habits, and those who knew him best recognized he had made such a drastic change that they were suspicious. I will assure you that any habit I break up I'll replace with better habits. That's a promise.

It is impossible to interfere with or suspend even for one second any of Nature's laws. Nature has a law of fixation. Individuals should have a law of fixation. They should fix in their minds the things they want and keep out the things they don't want. As a matter of fact, we are all afflicted by fixations. There are fixations or fears, and that's my business—to break up those fixations and replace them with other fixations more to your liking and more to your benefit.

In order to recondition your mind, you have to get on a different plane. Get yourself conditioned for success, happiness, health, and you will have to break a lot of habits.

CHAPTER TWO

Master Mind

May 21, 1947

We are on a grand subject tonight, the subject of the Master Mind. The Master Mind principle consists of an alliance of two or more minds working in perfect harmony for the attainment of a definite objective. That's about as brief a definition of the Master Mind that I can give. Let me say, however, that no one has ever attained outstanding success in any calling in the upper brackets of success without application of the Master Mind principle.

There are several fundamental principles in connection with this subject, and I'm going to break them down one at a time and reassemble them in a summary. The first principle is that the Master Mind principle is the medium through which one mind procures the full benefits of the experience, the training, and the specialized knowledge of other people, as completely as if they were one's own. Isn't it a marvelous thing to recognize that there is a means by which you may take full and complete advantage of the brains of other people—of their minds, their background, their influence, their knowledge—as completely as if you had those things yourself? There is such a principle, and there is such a method of taking advantage of and applying it to whatever end you may pursue.

Through the specialized knowledge of the geologist, for example, one may understand the structure of this earth without any training in geology, and through the experience and knowledge of the chemist one may make practical use of chemistry without having training in chemistry. Through the use of the Master Mind principle, one may take full and complete benefit of all of the sciences, or of any of them, without being familiar with them in the slightest. Evidence of that may be found in the work of Mr. Thomas A. Edison, who had only three months of formal schooling in his entire life, and yet in his work as an inventor he made use in one way or another of all of the natural sciences.

I know there is in this audience a vast number of men and women who have ideas they would like to carry out but do not have the courage because they feel deficient as to some form of knowledge that they may need. Perish the idea that you can't carry out that idea you possess, because through the Master Mind principle you can take full benefit of the knowledge or education of other people.

Second, an active alliance of two or more minds in a spirit of perfect harmony for the attainment of a common objective stimulates each mind to a higher degree of concentration than that ordinarily experienced and paves the way for that state of mind known as Faith. That's an important factor to bear in mind. Whenever two minds come together in a Master Mind alliance, each is stimulated to a higher plane, where it tunes in to a higher knowledge than is available on the lower plane.

The third: A Master Mind alliance, properly conducted, stimulates each mind to move with enthusiasm, personal initiative, imagination, and creativity to a degree far above that which the average individual experiences in moving without such an alliance. You know, of course, that enthusiasm is one of the most important things. You couldn't be very convincing as a salesman, a speaker, an orator, a lawyer, if you didn't put enthusiasm back of your words.

The fourth premise: To be effective, a Master Mind alliance must be active. That's highly important. It must be active. It cannot be passive. The mere association of minds is not enough. They must engage in pursuit of a definite purpose and must move with perfect harmony. Without that factor of perfect harmony, the alliance may be nothing more than ordinary cooperation or friendly coordination of effort, which is something vastly different from the Master Mind. Ordinary coordination of effort is called cooperation, and the difference between cooperation and the Master Mind consists entirely in this element of complete and perfect harmony. I can give you a lot of illustrations of cooperation which gained power but nothing to compare with the power the same relationship of people could develop based on the Master Mind. Take, for instance, a company of soldiers, military men, working under orders. There is perfect coordination but not always perfect harmony.

The fifth premise: It is a matter of established record that all individual successes based upon any kind of achievement above mediocrity are attained through the Master Mind principle. Most successes are the result of personal power, and personal power of such proportions as to enable one to rise above mediocrity is not attained without the application of the Master Mind principle.

Now I'll start giving you some illustrations of what constitutes the Master Mind in action. One of the finest examples I can call to your attention is that of Franklin D. Roosevelt when he was first elected to the presidency in 1933—the method which he used to induce the American people to supplant fear with faith. I had the privilege of sitting in on this and studying it very carefully. I watched everything that happened and had the privilege of helping to build one of the most outstanding Master Mind alliances this country has ever known. I'll tell you what that consisted of and how it operated.

You know, of course, when Mr. Roosevelt went into office, the people of the country were in a state of fear—a stampede of fear—selling their property, stocks, bonds, and what have you for whatever they could get for them. It was actually a Master

Mind between the people of the United States in reverse gear—a Master Mind based on fear. Mr. Roosevelt stepped in, and if ever there was a man suited to take control, he was, because he had the necessary qualifications, the temperament, to reverse the minds of the people and start them thinking in terms of achievement and recovery instead of business depression.

I wonder if there are many people in the United States who know how that was done? He had a Master Mind of a great number of people, without whom he could not have accomplished what he did in stopping the stampede. The restoration of confidence was the work of at least 100 men working according to a definite plan.

First of all, we had a plan whereby both houses of Congress worked in harmony with the president to the very last man. They forgot about party lines, and for one time they started thinking and acting as American citizens and not politicians. Wouldn't it be a grand thing if they would do that all the time? It makes one sick at heart to observe how some of those men whom we have sent to Washington to represent us actually damage us because of their friction and lack of cooperation of effort.

Both houses of Congress worked for the good of the people and, using a definite objective in mind, they followed this plan to the last letter, and you know what that definite objective was? It was to restore the confidence of the people in the country—nothing else except that in the beginning. Then we worked out a plan whereby the majority of the newspaper publishers of the country, regardless of their political affiliations, worked together and began to take the scare headlines off the front pages of the paper and write about things that would restore the confidence of the people. They started talking in terms of prosperity, recovery, the restoration of businesses, and the things that were really constructive; and in a little while, the newspapers had the people talking in the same terms. People are very greatly influenced by headlines. We all are.

Third, we had the radio broadcasters squarely back of the administration, putting into the minds of the people the positive and not the negative. There is no telling how many people we reached, but we know it was a lot.

And fourth: All religions, including the Jews, the Catholics, and the Protestants, got behind this movement and worked together, regardless of denomination. Wouldn't it be fine if they did that all the time? Wouldn't it be a fine thing if there were no denominations? One of the damaging things is that it separates people. That's why I don't have any religious affiliations, no political affiliations. I feel we are all brothers and sisters—Americans first, last, and always.

Fifth, the leaders of both major political parties got behind the administration. I am not talking about the rank and file; I am talking about the leaders, Republican and Democrat alike. If they hadn't gotten behind the president, there would have been no stopping of the stampede, no restoration of confidence in the quick time that it was done in.

I have often said that when we elect a man president, he is our president for four years whether we believe in his policies or not, and it would be far better if we were to get behind and help him be a good president than to knife him in the back. Look what happened when Mr. Truman went into office. We were so fed up and so tired of the way things had been going that we said, "Now we are going to get some relief from all the strikes and what have you." Without leadership, without anyone sending out a call, the people of the United States seemed to unite in all their thoughts. And I am sure Mr. Truman had the majority of the people back of him, praying for him, hoping for him and wishing that he would be a good president, with the result that he started off like a house afire. If he had had the millstones out from around his neck, I daresay he would have made a fine president, but he didn't have as good a chance as he would have had had he been elected by the people of the United States. He was really an appointed president, a president by accident, with loads of millstones around his neck, so he couldn't act on his own 100 percent. But in spite of that, the people were pulling for him, and it really and truly gave him a good start, a fine opportunity.

I have seen men come into a new job and be doomed from the first because the employees took a disliking to them. And when that condition arises, the man might as well get out.

On the other hand, I have seen where a man came in with the approval of the employees, and he immediately became a bigger, more efficient man as the result of that support. I have never known a man to be president of the United States—and I have known them all from Theodore Roosevelt up to this time—that he didn't immediately become a bigger and stronger man after his election. The job lifted the man up. What President Franklin Roosevelt did is a fine illustration of what the Master Mind can do. Most of you are old enough to remember the condition in 1933 when chaos prevailed throughout this nation, and you all remember how quickly things changed. People were attracted to believing in terms of recovery instead of believing in fear—all the result of using those five sources of influence, all of which were needed in the crisis of that time.

Another illustration of the Master Mind operating on a huge scale was that of Andrew Carnegie and his staff. Mr. Carnegie didn't know anything about the making or distributing or selling of steel and didn't pretend to, but he had in his organization men who, in their combined knowledge, knew all that was known at that time about making and distributing steel, and they aided him. When Mr. Carnegie first entered the steel business, steel was selling at $140 a ton, which made it prohibitive for a great many building purposes. He went to work, and as a result of the combined knowledge of some 20 men, they whittled the price of steel down to around $20 per ton and thereby made the modern skyscraper and the modern bridge possible.

Mr. Carnegie was one of the most adept men in the use of the Master Mind principle I have ever had the privilege of knowing. His entire fortune and achievement were due to the knowledge of those men, and here's what he said about his relations with them: "My job is to keep those men working together in a spirit of harmony, and it is very difficult, for it is very difficult to get even two people to agree on anything for five minutes." And we all know that is true.

I can give you an illustration of one of his Master Mind allies, his chief chemist. He said he wanted the best chief chemist in the world and sent a scout, and he looked all over the world and finally found him in the great Friedrich Alfred Krupp working in Germany. He entered into a contract with him on a five-year basis, and before the end of the first year he had to fire him and pay him off for his full five years. The reason was that he was so temperamental he could not work in harmony with the rest of the Master Mind alliance. He kept them in a state of upheaval all the time, and Mr. Carnegie realized that it would be fatal to keep him; and he paid him off and sent him back.

Mr. Carnegie also told me that one man with a negative attitude turned loose in an organization of 1,000 people could discolor the minds of the rest of them without opening his mouth and saying a word. That statement is very significant, and I want to dwell on it. If it is true that one man in an organization of 1,000 people can discolor the minds of the rest without opening his mouth and saying anything, how do you suspect he does it? There must be a reason for that. There must be a medium of his mind reaching the minds of the other men. What do you think that medium is? It's the medium of telepathy. Your mind is constantly in tune with every mind within its electrical range, whatever that range happens to be. Some minds have a much longer range than others. You are constantly picking up the thoughts of other people and often mistaking them for your own thoughts. That's the reason why you can't afford to remain in a negative atmosphere unless you are adept at protecting your mind from those negatives.

A Master Mind alliance of people thinking alike and working together in harmony, without jealousy, practically creates one mind that is available to every individual within that alliance. You can see why it is important to have harmony—because the moment there is a lack of harmony in one mind, it breaks the entire chain.

The author of this philosophy is a fine illustration of the Master Mind alliance. This Master Mind alliance consisted in the collaboration of some 500 top-ranking men of America who worked with me over a long period of time in a spirit of perfect harmony for the organizing of this philosophy. It wouldn't have been possible for one man to give the world this philosophy during a lifetime if he hadn't had access to that Master Mind alliance. It was made possible through Mr. Carnegie.

I want to tell you something about that alliance. I had to sell myself to over 500 men, and I never had one of them refuse me, in spite of the fact that they were all very busy and regarded their time as valuable. I couldn't have gotten to them except for Mr. Carnegie's assistance. Despite the fact that they were so busy, I got all the cooperation, all the time, I needed, and I got it without money. I want to impress that upon you, because somewhere along the line you are going to be in the position I was in when I started out with Mr. Carnegie. You're going to be in a position where you want powerful influence. And you want to know how to get that, don't you?

There are many ways, all of them based on some combination of motives. Nobody does anything without a motive. I'll tell you what the motive was that I used when I approached a man to collaborate with me on the building of this philosophy. If I wrote him a letter, I started out something like this:

> Dear Mr. Ford:
>
> I have been commissioned by Mr. Andrew Carnegie to engage in some twenty years of research for the purpose of uncovering the causes of success and failure in the lives of individuals. I have come to you for help because of the long years of rich experiences you have had in your business.
>
> It will be necessary for me to contact you on a great number of occasions and take up considerable of your time which I hope you will willingly give, and I am sure that you will when I tell you that I am asking this collaboration not on behalf of myself,

but on behalf of the people of the world, some of whom are not yet born.

And then I said:

> This cooperation will not be worth to you the three-cent stamp I am putting on this letter, but it may mean the difference between success and failure to many a worthy man and woman who will contact this philosophy based on your experience, then believe in it and succeed by it.

Do you see what a position that put him in? Had you ever thought that most people will do something to help somebody else when they wouldn't do it to help you when you asked it?

I want to tell you something else about this business of getting cooperation. I want to pass on to you the technique that will enable you to get through life as successfully as I'm getting through life now. I want to give you the full benefit of my entire experience in connection with selling myself, because no matter what you are doing, you will come to the point very soon when you will want to make application of this philosophy of selling your services, your merchandise, your products, your ideas, or whatever it is you want to get across, and you will need the cooperation of other people in order to do it. Salesmanship is an important thing. We all have to be salespeople, and we are all salespeople, although we are not always efficient salespeople.

I had a woman come to see me this morning. She wanted to start a Master Mind alliance with me. She started to tell me all her difficulties. She was blind and started in by giving me a summary of her background for the past 20 years. She used to work for the movies, had considerable money invested in a movie concern. It was all lost. Her husband started drinking. She lost her mother in death. She had troubles with her relatives. She gave me an outline of her difficulties for the past 20 years. There was not one constructive thing that happened. And then she said, "Now. Dr. Hill, why do you think my eyes went bad on me?" I said, "You are lucky to be able to talk to me with all your negative attitude. Your attitude is enough to attract everything that you don't want. I hope you know I don't mean to be harsh with you, but I'm not a bit surprised that your husband drinks. It's a wonder that he doesn't leave home and not live at that address."

She said, "What can I do to stop him?" And I said, "You can't do anything, but you can do something to help yourself. You've been thinking about your losses, and the more you do that, the more you attract other losses. Quit thinking about your losses, make up your mind you are going to benefit by your experience, and then adopt as your definite major purpose in life that you are going to center your thoughts on the restoration of your sight. Keep your mind so filled with the belief that you are going to see again that the optical nerve will be restored. The first thing you know, your husband will stop drinking, your relatives will stop abusing you, and when you get into that definite frame of mind, come to see me again and I can do something for you, because before I can do anything for you, you must do something for yourself."

The reason I repeat that is because I want to say the same thing to you. You don't have a tale of woe like that, I know, but the first thing for you to do is to start a Master Mind alliance between you and a positive person who recognizes no such thing as defeat, and start cultivating that person and start preparing yourself for the execution and the application of this philosophy. And when you have done a good job of working on yourself, you will find the philosophy will work much better. You will attract people who will cooperate with you willingly, and you won't have to work any harder than I did when I went out to get the cooperation of those 500 men. I knew before I got there that those men were going to collaborate, that each was going to do precisely what I wanted him to do. I sold myself that idea. Whatever you are doing, before you ask anybody to help you, make up your mind that you have the right to that cooperation. Sell yourself the idea that it's right before you ask anyone else.

Now, I am going back to something I wanted to tell you a while ago. I hope you will understand me when I say that I can get anything in this world that I want. I want you to know that you are in partnership with me. I want you to know that you are in good company for the simple reason that I can get anything I want. If I can get it for myself, I can get it for you, can't I?

When I start out to get something, it is of very great importance that I get an affirmative answer from the man I approach. I don't go at it directly. I perhaps send out an emissary and find out just exactly what his attitude is going to be. Then I go to see him, and I know how to approach him. I know what his objections are going to be, if any, and I have it worked out before I arrive.

Let's say I want to borrow $100,000, or maybe $1,000. I don't just walk into the bank and tell them, "I'm Napoleon Hill, and I need $1,000." Instead, I probably would become acquainted with the particular official from whom I wanted to get that money, and before I said anything about that, I would sell him on the great possibilities of what I am trying to do. I would let him know I have a fine reason to want the money, and then I would be almost sure to get it. Incidentally, I have borrowed money just that way and have had the bank voluntarily offer to lend me money when I didn't need it.

All of which adds up to the fact that whatever you are going to do in connection with the Master Mind principle, you have got to condition your own mind, otherwise you are not going to succeed. And when you find yourself negative, don't under any circumstances try to operate with the Master Mind members while you are negative. Get out of their presence and stay out until you make yourself positive. If you don't, the same thing will happen to your group that Mr. Carnegie said would happen when you turn a man loose in an organization with a negative mind. States of mind are communicative. There are certain diseases that we know are communicative like measles and whooping cough, but it has never occurred to many of us that mental states are communicative. And if you want to relate yourself to other people, be sure the things you are passing on to them are positive and not negative, because they are going to reflect back the state of mind you are passing on to them.

Mrs. Hill and I have had some very marvelous experiences in connection with this business of conditioning the mind. In the community we live in, there are two drug stores. Both have lunch counters, and when we first came here two years ago, we often went into one where the lunch counter was operated by a woman. And we saw her get into an argument, almost hair pulling, many times. We never have been in that place that we didn't see her get into an argument. We marveled at her tendency to fly off the handle and be unpleasant to the customers. But we made up our minds that she was not going to act that way toward us and we were not going to resent her, and the very moment we would go in there her whole face would change, even though she might be in the midst of an argument with a customer. She would change her whole mental attitude. The head of the chain of drug stores probably would give a great deal of money to know how to condition the minds of his people to be pleasant toward their customers. The whole secret was that we made up our minds not to be severe on her but to adjust her to our mental state. Without her knowing it, we set up a little Master Mind alliance between Mrs. Hill and her and I, and the dominating minds were the ones that prevailed. Bear that in mind in connection with your Master Mind: it is always the strongest ones that prevail.

I am sure that woman doesn't know to this date why it was that she received us with such kindness. We didn't leave big tips on the counter. We weren't bribing her. We just held the right state of mind. It is highly important in this philosophy to condition your mind so that when you speak, not only will your words be heard, but the feeling behind your words will go along with it. It is not always the words but the mental attitude in which you speak. I have tried this out many times, and being a very fast speaker, I get excited sometimes and there have been times when nobody could possibly follow what I said, but the audience applauded, and although they didn't know what I said, they knew the spirit in which it was said.

> *Condition your mind so that when you speak, not only will your words be heard, but the feeling behind your words will go along with it.*

Mr. and Mrs. Henry Ford had the most outstanding Master Mind alliance I have ever had the privilege of tuning in on. Mrs. Ford was largely responsible for his success. I have every reason to believe that if it hadn't been for her influence, patience, consideration, understanding, and sympathy, he would never have gotten on the road to success. It was her influence on the personality of Henry Ford that caused him to develop and grow. There was never any lack of harmony. There was always complete and perfect harmony in all their relations.

There was another Master Mind of equal importance between Mr. and Mrs. Edison. Although Mrs. Edison was not an inventor, she probably knew as much about each invention as her husband did. No matter how late he came home from the laboratory, she was always up and waiting on him when he came home, and she had to have a report of his day, good or bad. You can't fail with a wife like that. I want to remind you of that. If you have complete singleness of purpose with the woman you marry, I want to tell you there is nothing you can't succeed in. If you don't have it, you have almost three strikes against you, and it works the other way around, ladies. You must have harmony and cooperation from your husband. It must not be a one-way purpose; it must be a two-way purpose.

There are two general types of Master Mind alliances. I want you to understand the difference between these. One is the alliance for purely business or professional advantages, consisting of individuals who have a motive of material or financial nature—in other words, a purely monetary alliance, you might say, designed to help you sell your personal services, your skill, your ability, or to help you succeed in business. That's one type. The other type is for purely social and personal reasons, consisting of one's relatives (some of them), friends, and religious advisors, where no material gain is sought. The most important, of course, is the Master Mind alliance between a man and his wife.

These are the two general types, and you need not only one group, but both groups, because there are different motives back of each. Your Master Mind allies chosen for your business group should be chosen for their ability to help you get to where you are going. The allies in the other group may be chosen on the basis of liking the people.

There are some people I like that other people don't like—some people who are not very successful, not very ambitious, and don't have the goodwill and confidence of their closest relatives, yet I like them because of certain influences they have on me. I have friends in almost all walks of life, in the highest and lowest places, because it is my business to understand human nature, and in order to do that I have to keep those close alliances with people in all walks of life. I can't hope to bring them over to my way of thinking, nor is it my business to do that. I want to study them as they are. By their very nature, many of them are not fit for my Master Mind group. You should have a close association with people who have an inspirational effect on you in your personal group, and if you have people who do not give you more confidence, more faith, more courage, you had better get rid of them.

When you have arranged rapport between your mind and the minds of others, you will find that it will inspire ideas that will come to the other people and to you. In other words, when the Master Mind is in effect, it produces other ideas than would come to you at other times. I have had the experience many times of sitting down and talking with government officials—for instance, the meeting I had with the attorney general of the United States and his staff when Franklin Roosevelt was in office. They wanted to stop the kidnapping rackets. I sat and listened, but I had no ideas at all. However, I did have an open mind. And after the last person had finished speaking, it was time for me to be called upon in just a matter of seconds, and I knew that when I got up, I was going to wash out. But in a matter of seconds, the whole answer came to me. And that answer was to have a law passed to bribe the associates of No. 1 criminals so that they could turn them in at a price. That law was passed, and almost overnight the kidnapping racket went out of existence. I speak of this to show you how the mind works when among friendly minds.

I want to tell you about one of my students who came up and said, "I would like for you to give us a concrete illustration of how to condition the mind." Isn't that a good question? She sprang a good one on me. I intended to get to that a little later on, but this is just as good a day as any.

Sometime ago, it became evident to me that I was going to have to have a new set of dentures; and if you don't think it requires mind conditioning to get around to having that done, it's because you haven't had it done. I took some three months to condition my mind for that job. I followed the technique of sitting down and writing out a complete list of every benefit that I would get out of the transaction, thoroughly familiarizing myself with the positive side of the whole operation. First thing I said: "Think what it would do to your appearance. It will take ten years off your age." Who wouldn't go through an ordeal like that to reduce his age? "Secondly, it is going to add to your physical health and change your mental attitude. And third, it is going to eliminate entirely one negative thought that keeps occurring in your mind—that you are going to have to have those dentures made—because you will never have to have it done again."

There are 15 or 20 other advantages, and I wrote them down and so thoroughly sold myself that when the doctor gave me the anesthetic, there was no fear. And while he was pulling my teeth my mind was concentrating on the radio program that I was going to give the next Sunday. And finally, I was aware of the fact that the doctor was fooling around in my mouth, and I said, "Doctor, when are you going to start pulling?" And he said, "I have them all out but one."

When you go to condition your mind for anything, make a list of all the benefits you are going to get out of it; then sell yourself those benefits and keep your mind off the opposite.

Now we come to the general instructions for the forming and maintenance of the Master Mind alliance, and here they are. The first thing is to adopt a definite purpose as an objective to be obtained by the alliance, choosing individual members whose education, experience, and influence are such as to make them of the greatest value. There isn't any use in forming a Master Mind alliance just to have somebody to chat with. It will soon fail if you don't have action or a motive behind it. You might have a second motive. It might be to build up a pleasant relationship, friendship, and also to have you succeed in your job or calling. You should choose people who have the ability, the personality, and the willingness to cooperate with you. Just remember that you must plant in the minds of these allies a motive. They must benefit.

You know what keeps friendship alive? Had you ever thought of that? There is only one way you can do it: You have to be a friend and keep on being one. You have to keep in contact with your friends: call them on the telephone, go to see them, invite them to lunch, keep up that continuous contact. If you let it die down for a few weeks, you will begin to lose that friendship. In the Navy, contact is a very important thing. The ships have to keep constant contact with the flagship. It should be so in our life.

Second, determine what appropriate benefit each person may receive in return for cooperation in the Master Mind alliance. When you do that, make yourself very familiar with the nine basic motives we discussed last week. In the business alliance you may be very sure what the motive will be. Monetary gain, profit. If you are going out to make some profit, be willing to divide it with those who help you. Be not only fair but generous with them, and the more generous you are with them, the more help you will get from them. What a pity all businessmen don't know about that! Before I'm through, I hope they will.

Incidentally, on that point, it just occurs to me that the turning point in Henry Ford's life came in 1914 when I influenced him to adopt the famous $5 a day wage scale as a means of his going the extra mile with his employees.

Next, establish a definite place where the alliance will meet, and arrange a definite time for the mutual discussion of the plan. Don't just leave it to chance. Indefiniteness will bring defeat. Keep a regular means of contact between all members of this alliance. Keep all of them working in enthusiastic regular meetings.

You can start out with a plan that is very good, but before you are through discussing it you will modify that plan until eventually you have the perfect plan. The round table discussion will be the place where everyone meets, where everybody speaks with confidence. They all see what's on the table. You have no secrets, and thereby you gain the full benefit of each member of the Master Mind. It's the burden of the leader to see that harmony prevails among all members and that action is maintained constantly.

That word *action* is very important. You know when you get up in the morning not feeling so good, maybe you didn't eat the right kind of food the day before or have the right kind of drink either—whatever the cause, you don't feel so good. You couldn't lay your hand on any part of the body that complains, but you are just not full of pep. You know what is a very fine remedy for that? Just get a hoe and work in the garden till you start perspiring. Fast action is a very fine thing. I take mine out in walking. I write books, write lectures, create ideas, work out problems for my students, all while I am by myself, and then I find the ideas begin to grow. I carry a pad and a pencil in my pocket and start writing as fast as they come. You have to have a technique, and I am now giving you an important part of it.

The watchword behind the alliance should be definiteness of purpose backed continuously by perfect harmony. The number of individuals in an alliance should be governed by its nature and purpose. Very often I am asked how many members should serve. That depends entirely on what the purpose is. If you were going into a purpose like Mr. Edison's, you would have to have a stupendous number. If you are going into a lesser undertaking, you may have a smaller number. The nature and purpose will entirely determine the size of that alliance. I can say the fewer you have, the better off you will be because there will be less chance of friction. Two can get along better than three and three better than four or five. So, the fewer you have in your organization, the better the chance for maintaining perfect harmony.

I want to give you an outline of the Master Mind principle as it interlocks with certain other principles, and there are seven of them. The first one, number one, is Definiteness of Purpose. That's the first thing you have to deal with in creating and maintaining a Master Mind for any purpose.

Second, there must be Personal Initiative. In other words, you must take the lead. You can't wait for somebody else to come along and help you out. In building this philosophy, I had to find out first of all who had the knowledge, and then I had to go after them. I had to take the initiative, then go to the necessary expense—sometimes travel all the way across the country—in order to get to a man whose collaboration I needed.

Third, Applied Faith. There couldn't be a Master Mind within the meaning of that word where there is no applied faith.

The fourth principle is that of Going the Extra Mile. You will be surprised when you follow the habit of going the extra mile how easy it will be for you to get cooperation from other people. The fact that you are in that frame of mind where you are willing to do that will mean other people will want to cooperate with you.

The fifth factor: Organized Effort. You must have plans back of what you want to do. You can't just develop a Master Mind alliance and have it succeed except as it operates through definite and organized plans.

Sixth: Self-Discipline. You will not have a Master Mind alliance unless you discipline yourself. Don't try to discipline others, but discipline yourself, and by that I mean complete and full discipline in every sense of the word. One of the forms of discipline will be to keep things focused, especially when you are discussing the achievement of your major purpose. Don't let other things distract your attention.

The seventh is almost as important: Controlled Attention. You can't succeed in life doing a dozen things at the same time. I don't know anybody who can do even two things at the same time and do them well. You have to concentrate on one thing. And a lifetime is entirely too short a time unless you learn the art of concentrating, keeping yourself focused and not weakening for even one step in any way.

CHAPTER THREE

Going The Extra Mile

June 4, 1947

Before I start, I want to ask a question. I want to ask you to think about this question very seriously before you answer it, and I would like to have you answer truthfully to yourself as well as to me; answer conscientiously. I want to know how many people there are in this class who really and truly can say that they have adopted and applied the principle of Going the Extra Mile in their work every day?

I appeared before a group of rubber workers in the Rubber Men's Club last night; and when I put that question to them, they all looked around and grinned sheepishly. And about 15 or 20 raised their hands, and I said, "Go on, all of you, raise your hands. It doesn't hurt to do a little lying now and then. I have done that myself."

Now, I want to ask you one more question: How many in this class think it really and truly pays to go the extra mile and intend to keep on doing that?

I want to tell you, my friends, if I had to choose one of the 17 principles of success and rest my chances on that principle alone, I would, without hesitation, choose Going the Extra Mile, because that is the one where I can make myself indispensable to other people. *Indispensable* is the word—you should look it up and write it down in your consciousness, because if you are ever to occupy very much space in the world, you will have to make yourself indispensable to a great many people.

Someone has said there is no such thing as an indispensable man, but so far as you, as an individual, are concerned, it is not true. I like to think I am indispensable to a great many millions of people. I know I am indispensable to Annie Lou. She knows that too and admits it. When you get to the point where you are not concerned as to whether you are indispensable or not, you are treading on very dangerous ground.

> *If you are ever to occupy very much space in the world, you will have to make yourself indispensable to a great many people.*

I want to take you into some of the niceties of this business of applying the extra mile principle, but before I do that, I want to define the term and tell you exactly what that term means. It means that you are rendering more and better service than you are paid to render and that you are doing it all the time as a regular, established habit. You are doing it without regard to the attitude in which that service is received by anybody, and you will do it in a pleasant, pleasing, positive mental attitude. You will not do it grudgingly.

I had a student some time ago who heard me lecture on this subject of going the extra mile one time, and then he said, "I know exactly how I am going to cash in on that principle." He went to his employer and asked if he objected to him coming down on Sunday, and his employer said, "No." He said, "If there is a lot of work to be done, I would like to come down and help out." He did that on four Sundays and sent the employer a bill for time and a half for Sunday work. He missed the point entirely. He didn't get the spirit.

On the other hand, I have had a lot of experience with people who seem to have had circumstances occur in their lives that show this doesn't pay off. I had a circumstance like that with a group of railroad men working for one of the big railroad companies. They have been going out of their way to cut down accidents and have done a swell job, cutting them down approximately 40 percent, a savings of many dollars a year to the transportation company. Recently, their leader was called in and fired for going the extra mile because he ran afoul of another faction who didn't want him to make a better showing. Had he not been a student on his own account of this philosophy, he might have become very bitter and said, "As far as I am concerned, the philosophy of going the extra mile hasn't paid off," but he would have been wrong. And he didn't know that almost a month ago, I began to pull strings for the purpose of lifting him out of the railroad service and putting him in a much better job with the State Railroad Commission. And now that he has been fired, he will be able to come back, and instead of asking for permission to help the company out, he will give them directions. He will be in a much better position to direct them to carry out his ideas of safety. He will be earning more money, and the thing that caused me to intercede on his behalf was the fine spirit he showed of helping his fellow employees. The law was working on his behalf, and he didn't know it. I didn't tell him to stick to it and I would see that he got a better job. I have never in my life held out any promise of compensation to my students or anyone else for going the extra mile. I wanted my students to apply it because of the principle and not because of any promises from me.

Don't let anybody tell you going the extra mile doesn't pay off. It does if you watch your attitude. That is important—that mental attitude. Get into the habit of going the extra mile because of the pleasure you get out of it, because of what it does inside of you, and you may be sure it will do plenty.

A great many years ago, a young man by the name of Edwin Barnes got hold of this philosophy, and he chose as his definite purpose a partnership with a very great man, no less than the great Thomas A. Edison himself. When he broke the news to his young wife that he intended to go over to East Orange, New Jersey, and become a partner of Edison, she rushed over and put her hand on his head and said, "Edwin, are you sick?"

And he said, "No, why?" And she said, "You are talking out of your head," and he said, "What do you expect me to talk out of?" She said, "You don't have railroad fare," and he said, "No, but freight trains run there." She said, "What will he think of you coming in there like a tramp?" He said, "It doesn't make any difference what he thinks of me; it's what I think of him." Wouldn't it be a marvelous thing if all of you got that viewpoint where you felt that if you did something for a person, he is the one who is being favored? He is under obligation to you and not you under obligation to him?

Edwin Barnes intended to put Edison under obligation to him. Emerson had something to say on that. He said, "Put life itself in debt to you"—not in those words, but substantially the same meaning.

Barnes got on a freight train and went over there and walked right into the office and said, "I want to see Mr. Edison." And the secretary said, "What did you want to see him about?" And he said, "I am going to become his partner," and the secretary said, "I don't believe I have made any appointments for anyone to see Mr. Edison today, and I certainly don't know anything about anyone becoming his partner. Mr. Edison has no partners." Barnes said, "You may not know it, and he may not know it; but I know it, and I'm here to see him." By that time, a group of people in the outer office who had heard this conversation were standing around, and they saw Barnes with that suitcase which had been knocked around and his suit not pressed. And I expect he looked too funny for words, and they let out a laugh. He went on like he didn't hear it, and finally the secretary said, "The most I can do is to go back and see your future partner and see if he is ready to see you." Then he looked back and said, "Are you the junior partner or the senior partner?" And Barnes said, "It doesn't make any difference what my title is now."

In a little while, the secretary came back and said, "Mr. Edison said come back to his office; he would like to look you over." A half hour went by after Mr. Barnes went into Mr. Edison's office, and nothing happened. Three quarters of an hour, and nothing happened. And after an hour, the secretary and other employees got worried. They thought this tramp maybe had murdered Mr. Edison. And they formed a committee and went back there, and here is what they found. They found Ed Barnes down on his hands and knees scrubbing the floor of a storeroom. He had been there almost an hour at that, and the committee walked out. Mr. Edison walked in and said, "Young man, you have taken quite a while to clean this floor." Barnes said, "You took quite a while to invent the incandescent lamp, and as I remember it, you failed 10,000 times before you completed it, but you did do the job right, didn't you?" And Mr. Edison said, "I guess that's my answer; that answer will do."

The next thing the committee knew, Barnes was a handy man in the Edison plant. He went from one minor job to another until Mr. Edison completed the Ediphone dictation device. After that, Mr. Edison called a conference of his salesmen to have them take the invention out to the public. And they had been in discussion about three days, and not one of the men thought that anybody would buy it. One man said, "I know very well men are not going to dictate to a tin can. They prefer blondes." Then Barnes jumped up on the table—nobody knew how he got into the conference room—and he said, "It seems nobody here wants this machine. I can sell it. Let me do it." And in unison they yelled back, "Boy, you have got it."

It weighed about 50 pounds, and Barnes took it to New York and walked up and down Broadway day after day until he finally sold one machine. At the end of a month, he had sold eight machines. He went back and laid the orders on Mr. Edison's desk and said, "This proves beyond a doubt that this machine can be sold, and it is working and is being used, and all you have to do is increase the number of sales branches and spread it all over the United States." Edison said, "Young man, when you first came in here and announced that you were going to become my partner, everybody laughed at you except me, and I am not laughing at you now. I am congratulating you on having inside of you the stuff it takes to make a good partner." And the slogan of the firm today is "Made by Edison and installed by Barnes." Barnes has made himself immensely wealthy—many times a millionaire. He is the only partner the great Thomas A. Edison ever had.

From that story, can you tell me what made Barnes a partner of Edison? Edison had thousands of men working for him. Not one of them made the step up to become a partner. Not one of them made the millions out of the connection that Ed Barnes made, and so it means he had something the others didn't have. And if you can ferret out in yourselves, each of you, that something that young man had and turn the spotlight on that something, I want to tell you, you can equal his achievement. You may not aspire to becoming a millionaire, but you have some sort of an aspiration; and whatever it is, just remember there is a means of focusing favorable attention on yourself, and that is within your hands entirely. You don't have to ask anybody for the privilege of going the extra mile.

I fancy that the average man, when chided by his wife, as Barnes was, would have stopped right there. Or he would at least have said, "I'll not go over to see Mr. Edison until I can maneuver around and get a letter from some influential person." That would have shown a lack of confidence. He didn't lack it; he had it.

I will tell you something else that shows what can happen when you really and truly appropriate the principle of going that extra mile. When I met Mr. Barnes a great many years after he had become the partner of Edison, I found he had 31 suits, all tailor-made, all of imported cloth, and each one costing from $250 to $350 and some of them $400. His shoes were made to order. His cravats were made to order. All of his things were made to order, and he never wore the same outfit more than two days in one month. I thought I would have some fun with him, and I said, "When you get ready to throw away one of those suits, I wish you would let me know what trash barrel you are throwing it in." He said, "I bet you don't know why I have 31 suits, all of them made to order." I said, "I guess it is to feed your ego," and he said, "Well, let me tell you something, that day I stood before Thomas A. Edison and saw him scrutinize me from head to foot, I could tell just exactly what he was thinking, what was going through his mind. He was saying, 'What nerve this boy has, dressed as he is, to come in here.' So, I made up my mind as soon as I could afford it that no matter who I met or what circumstances I was in, I would know I was dressed better that he was from the skin out." And he said, "I don't care about the other people. I am not dressing for them. I am dressing for Ed Barnes."

Remember that in order to succeed, you need to build up your ego. If it is a new car or a new house you need, better not be too particular on that right now, but put it on the agenda for some future time. You will be surprised to know just what difference it will make to wash your automobile when it's dirty. When we got back from Yosemite this winter, it had been snowing and raining, and our car was dirty; and I don't like a dirty car. I washed it just as soon as I had a chance, and it purred like a kitty cat and ran better—made me feel better. I could do better work as a result of it.

I know why Ed Barnes had better clothes. He went the extra mile with himself in producing in his own mind the attitude that would enable him to hold that opportunity and make the most out of it. Remember, my friends, it is not very difficult to put yourself in the way of opportunity. And no matter what you want, if it is anything reasonable that you are entitled to, you can get it. I could probably point you very easily on the way to get it, but that would not be enough, for you would have to have the mental attitude to make yourself expect that opportunity and to make the most out of it after you got it.

It is not very difficult to put yourself in the way of opportunity.

I want to tell you that in my going the extra mile with Andrew Carnegie, I spent 20 years in organizing this philosophy long before I made a dime from it. I not only didn't make anything out of it, but it cost me money. I had research men looking up things, and it was costing me a lot of money. And I had to do a lot of pushing of myself to stay on the job for 20 years. It was no easy job, especially when my relatives were always needling me in another direction, calling me unflattering names. There were times when I began to think maybe they were right, but back of all the feeling of doubt, when I was trying to keep myself keyed up to a condition of faith, there was also that feeling that the day would come when I not only would justify the 20 years I had put into this, but I would be proud of myself that I had it in me to stay on the job. I don't think it had crystalized into faith, but it was hope, and I kept fanning that hope, pressing down on it, and keeping it alive. And finally came the time of the payoff, when I had the privilege, and do now have the privilege, of occupying more space in the world than any other author in the history of personal achievement literature.

When I say, "occupy more space," I want to give you some concrete examples of what has happened in the way of a payoff to show you that I am not speaking in the clouds, but speaking with both feet on the ground. After having spent 20 years acquiring this philosophy, if I wanted to write a new book, all I would have to do would be to give a publisher the title and outline the contents, and he would give me a contract for publication instantly. I say there is not an author today in the United States who wouldn't give a king's ransom if he could say that and it was true. Any publisher would take any book I would write and publish it, because I have established a reputation and a buying market, millions of people not only in this nation but in practically every nation in the world. And that field, incidentally, is growing by leaps and bounds.

Did it pay to go the extra mile for 20 years? I want to tell you, I wasn't smart enough to recognize what would happen in the beginning. My fondest expectations never led me beyond putting out one interpretation of the philosophy which would sell 100,000 copies. The average book sells less than 2,000 copies. One hundred thousand is considered wonderful. Why do my books sell better than others? Because 20 years of concentrated experience while I was going the extra mile went into them, and the reader picks that up and recognizes that. That's what makes the books sell.

I am calling that to your attention because just as sure as anything, those of you who are new to the philosophy will come to the place I did when you will feel that this business of going the extra mile sometimes pays off and sometimes does not. I want to tell you now that it always pays off and never lets you down and pays off in proportion to the intensity of how you apply it. I don't know how it does this or what causes it to be done, but I do know that before you get to the place in the application of this philosophy where it is paying off in terms of what you want in life, you will be tested many times. You will undergo sometimes a very severe series of tests, and remember when those testing times come that they are a great privilege because they give you an opportunity to make introspective inventory of yourself to see whether you have what it takes or not.

The last time I was forced to take inventory I wasn't so sure if I had what it took or not, and I was quite sure that if I hadn't had this philosophy, I wouldn't have made the grade. I was called upon to go the extra mile in a series of transactions which took all the willpower, every bit of faith I could muster, and out of that came my greatest gain to prove that this philosophy can do anything. It can with your help. The attitude you take toward it will be the determining factor.

My going the extra mile for 20 years with Andrew Carnegie I suppose did look foolish to my brother and my father and some of my other relatives who believed that I had taken 20 years out of my life at a time when I should have been making money. But there was one person in the world who didn't think it was foolish, and that was my stepmother. I only had one Master Mind ally to help me see it through. She said to me after I had attempted my first book and failed, "I don't attempt to be your psychic, but the time will come when you will be the greatest author of all time in your field." And I actually blushed because somehow I thought it couldn't be true.

I went back a little while ago to the place in Virginia where I was born. The house was gone. There was a pile of stones where what used to be the chimney had stood. It was a one-room house. We did everything in one room—ate there and slept there. I remember it so well. When they went to move to another mountain, I was just a little fellow, and they picked me up and put me on top of all our possessions in the wagon. And I remember so well looking into the future and saying to myself, "I suppose I will never be rich enough to have household items like this." I don't think I would ever have gotten out of those mountains if I hadn't applied this extra mile principle. I would be in those mountains now, probably making moonshine and killing rattlesnakes like some of my cousins who are there now.

I went back up there not long ago and called on all my relatives who I could find, and not one of them had changed.

They were living just like their ancestors had centuries ago. I came to the conclusion that had I not had a marvelous woman come into my home, I would still be there. She taught me the benefit of going the extra mile long before I came in contact with Andrew Carnegie. As a result of that, in every job I have ever had, I have made more money than anyone else made in that same job. At the age of 16 years, I was a manager in a coal mine because I had been taught not to stand around and wait for somebody to tell me what to do but to anticipate and jump right in and do it. That's what I mean by going the extra mile. Don't wait for people to have to tell you. That takes a lot of kick out of it. Tell yourself and jump in and do it.

As long as our system of government prevails and our free enterprise system exists, the greatest common asset available to the American people consists in their privilege of going the extra mile all the time, attracting opportunity, attracting cooperation, attracting a chance to promote themselves into whatever position in life they want.

> *The greatest common asset available to the American people consists in their privilege of going the extra mile all the time.*

The first half of this lecture I am devoting to the highlights of this philosophy. We come to the more prosaic part of it in the second half, but I want you to catch the spirit of the thing before we get down to the technique. There are certain things that you do in order to apply the principle of Going the Extra Mile, but those things would be useless unless you catch the spirit back of the thing.

If you have the right attitude in the things you do for people, you will put them under obligation. If you don't, they will hate you for doing things for them. Or they may not hate you, but they will at least dislike you and find an alibi for not reciprocating.

There is another thing in connection with going the extra mile, and I want to call it to your attention. Before you can accomplish anything very great in the world, you will have to have the cooperation of other people and will have to have the confidence of other people. If you have enough people who have confidence in you and in whom you have confidence, you can do almost anything. There is in this philosophy a technique which we call the swapping of favors, the borrowing of goodwill. You hear often of the goodwill of a business. A business will sell out and charge so much for buildings and equipment and, in addition to that, often charge several times the value of physical assets for goodwill. What do you think that means? It means the confidence that a great number of people have built up in that firm as a result of long years of satisfactory dealings.

You will have to the use of goodwill of other people; and if you don't learn how to get that goodwill in the shortest length of time, you are going to miss one of the greatest experiences in your entire life. There are two ways of getting the goodwill of other people. One: By a long series of satisfactory, honest relationships or dealings with those people. You can get it that way, but many of you have reached the point in life where you can't wait 15 or 20 years. You want it right now. You have plans to be carried out, and you want to move instantly.

There is one other thing you can do: you can borrow the goodwill of other people by swapping favors. We call that going the extra mile. You don't have to put him on notice that you are going to ask him to pay off. Circumstances may make it convenient for you to put him on notice, but generally speaking, don't. If you do something for a person, he doesn't usually say, "Now, what is this going to cost me?" If you don't do it in the right spirit, he will. He will say, "I have to watch my pocketbook because this guy wants something." You have to keep going the extra mile until you have established the confidence of that person. Oftentimes you have only to make known your needs and the other fellow will volunteer his cooperation. That's called swapping favors, and it is also related to the Master Mind.

Starting out, Arthur Brisbane was just a newspaper man, no better and no worse than thousands of other newspapermen. He might never have been heard from if he hadn't had a Master Mind alliance with Mr. William Hearst, the newspaper publisher. And Mr. Hearst, as a return favor for what Brisbane had done for him, put him and his column on the front page, and presto, Mr. Brisbane was made financially. He never in the world could have made the millions of dollars he did make, working by himself. If he hadn't put Mr. Hearst under obligation to him, he couldn't have done it.

"You scratch my back, and I'll scratch yours"—that's what I mean by this business of exchanging favors. In the exchanging of favors, who takes the initiative? Who extends the first favor? Suppose you want a favor from me. You want me to go out of my way to do something for you. Who takes the initiative? Yes, of course you take the initiative. By what? Asking me to do something for you? If you are smart, you don't do that. In the capacity of a student, you have the privilege, but if you wanted me to do something outstanding and you couldn't afford to have me say "no," what would you do? Yes, you would put me under obligation. You would be very careful about how you went about it.

You have heard me speak of my association with Mr. Robert G. LeTourneau of Georgia; and when it comes to this business of swapping favors, you will catch on to what I mean. The LeTourneau Company thinks they sought me out, but long before that I sought out the LeTourneau Company and planted one of my students there. And when they got into difficulties, I had friends at court and they sent for me. The fact of the matter is, I knew a year and a half before they sent for me that I was going to be there. I laid my plans accordingly.

I went the extra mile by inviting the key man into my class, giving him his tuition, giving him interview after interview. He was to be my contact at the LeTourneau Company. The hours I spent would have amounted to $1,250 in compensation if I had charged my regular rate, but I didn't. I was putting him under obligation so that when the time came when I wanted to go into the LeTourneau Company, I had put them under obligation. This man offered to pay me. I refused to take one penny because I was going to get a lot more than that. I want you to remember that a lot of times by refusing to take a conventional fee and biding your time and rendering more service, the time will come when your payoff will be very much more than the conventional sum.

Don't be afraid to keep up this business of going the extra mile. If the charges seem to be running too high against the other fellow, don't worry, because time does the collecting for every person who goes the extra mile. In time it will not only pay off the principal, but it will pay off compound interest upon compound interest. And another thing, if the compensation doesn't come from the particular person or persons for whom you go the extra mile, it will come from others. And very often it does come from other people whom you have never seen and never expect to see.

There is a strange thing about this business of going the extra mile, and that is the law of compensation, which has been explained so carefully by Emerson. This law of compensation is externally working, and it sees to it that everything you have rendered is paid for and also every penalty that should have been visited upon you also is visited upon you. It never makes mistakes. It is an individual system of accounting that keeps up with you and your affairs.

I want to give you an outline of the reasons or motives that you will have for going the extra mile—a catalog of them—so you will understand what they are. You will see then that nobody but an irresponsible person, or a person who doesn't have any ambition or enthusiasm, or an indifferent person, would refrain from going the extra mile after he has this catalog.

First: Going the extra mile places the law of increasing returns back of one. That means that the quality of the service that you give out and the quantity will come back to you in greatly multiplied form, just as, for example, the law of increasing returns works in the farmer's favor when he plants a seed of wheat in the ground, having first gone the extra mile by preparing the soil and planting this seed in the right season. After he has done that, for which he gets no pay, then Nature takes over and hands him back that grain of wheat and, in addition to that, 100 other grains to compensate him for his intelligence, thereby showering upon him the benefits of the law of increasing returns.

Everything you do in the way of rendering service places behind you this same law. If you render service which is worth $100, the chances are that eventually you will get back not only that $100 but ten times that quantity if you render this service in the right mental attitude. It may not come back in dollars but in increased opportunity for you to get ahead—promotion or the making of a new friend or group of friends. It may come back to you in a great variety of forms, all of which represent the law of increasing returns. If you neglect to go the extra mile, or don't even go the first mile, or go in a negative attitude in order to get an immediate compensation, the chances are that the law of diminishing returns will work and you will get back very much less or possibly nothing at all.

I don't know who made the law; all I know is that it works, and I learned how to make it work—learned which button to put my finger on to get the right reaction.

The second benefit is that it brings one to the favorable attention of those who can and do provide opportunity for self-promotion. It turns the spotlight of favorable attention on you.

Third: It tends to make one indispensable—to permit one to become indispensable in many different relationships—and therefore enables one to command more than average compensation. You will never command more than average compensation until you become indispensable to somebody or some group of somebodies.

> You will never command more than average compensation until you become indispensable to somebody.

Fourth: It leads to mental growth and physical perfection in the various forms of service, thereby developing greater ability and skill in one's chosen vocation. When you do a thing with the attitude that you are going to surpass the previous time, each time you really are growing. And I never went before a student body or a public audience in my life that I didn't intend to do better than I had ever done before. Sometimes I may fall down, but I never fall down so far as the effect on me is concerned. It helps me, of course. It is a healthy state of mind to intend to exceed your own record every time you make a move. Anything short of that is not healthy. Slowing down on the job, spending a little more time in the washroom. "I'm not getting enough pay. If I can't get it out of his purse, I'll take it out of his hide." That attitude doesn't pay off. And sometimes I will admit there are relationships where you feel you should take something out of his hide, but don't do it. Let somebody else do that. Give the best you have and learn to like it. You will be surprised how it will attract people to you.

Five: Going the extra mile protects one against the loss of employment and places one in a position to choose his own job and working conditions and attract new promotional opportunities. That alone would justify one in adopting this principle, especially one who is working for a salary. It enables you to occupy whatever space you want to in life. You don't have to ask anybody. Of course, if you belong to some unions, you would be discouraged, but there are a lot of ways of hitting a harder hammer blow or hitting two hammer blows instead of one, and sooner or later somebody is going to find out about that.

If you are in any kind of relationship where you don't feel free to go the extra mile, there is always such a thing as the old mother bird, Nature, pushing you out of the nest and making you find a better job some other place. These railroad boys I spoke of, when their leader became discouraged, he left, and he doesn't feel blue now, because he had a preview of the benefits that are coming to him. You will learn that every adversity carries with it the seed of an equivalent benefit, if you are ready to receive that benefit. You have to be in the right mental attitude to receive before you can benefit by it. If the fired railroad man had become bitter and wanted to go out and blow up the tracks because he had lost his job, there would have been no seed of an equivalent benefit for him. And some people are like that. Instead of looking for the equivalent benefit, they begin to look for an alibi, somebody to blame. You will never get anywhere looking for alibis. Always assume 100 percent blame, even though it was somebody else's mistake. It was your mistake because you didn't use all the ingenuity, all the strategy you could to avoid it.

> *Every adversity carries with it the seed of an equivalent benefit.*

Six: It enables one to profit by the law of contrast, because the majority of people do not practice the habit but follow the opposite by trying to get things they are not entitled to. If there has ever been a period in the history of the world where the majority of people are trying to get somewhere for nothing, it is today. When you see a person rendering service that is greater in quality and quantity than he is being paid for, he is in such fine contrast that you take notice of him, especially if you are his employer. You may not want to let him know that you recognize that. You may sidle around a little bit, but you might just as well not, because you are going to have to pay off sooner or later or your competitor is going to get that man.

An example of that is Henry Ford. At a time when there were no labor unions and hence no pressure was brought to bear, he voluntarily raised the wages of his employees to $5 a day, a 100 percent increase. I think I told you I had the privilege of writing out that plan, and incidentally it was the turning point in the financial life of Mr. Ford. His real success started in 1914. The vast majority of industrialists at that time prophesied that he would go broke within a year. What happened was that Mr. Ford's labor cost was far less because every man practically became his own supervisor. He didn't want to take a chance on losing that fat job, because he knew he couldn't get another one like it down the street. He put more into that job. He changed his mental attitude. And incidentally, the best labor in the country flocked to Henry Ford. His labor turnover declined. It paid him in a thousand ways. It paid in his reputation with the public because people wanted to buy a Ford instead of a Chevrolet or something else.

Seven: It leads to development of a pleasing mental attitude, which is among the more important traits of a pleasing personality. Isn't that a marvelous thing to recognize, that this changes your mental attitude and makes it pleasing, enabling you to attract people to you without making demands on them or asking them for anything? Look around you, and take inventory of the people you know, and convince yourself. Better still, start tomorrow and prove beyond a question of doubt that it is true. You can get anyone to act toward you the way you want them to act. That's a little trick that's worth knowing, isn't it? How do you get somebody to act toward you the way you want them to act? You do it by first acting toward him that way. Then, if he doesn't respond the first time, what do you do—quit? No, you go on and on and on. And then when you finally convince yourself that it is wrong and nothing happens, only then do you quit and move on.

There is another principle in this philosophy: personal initiative—doing the thing that needs to be done without somebody telling you what to do. I needn't go further without telling you that oftentimes you have to build a fire under this principle to cause something to happen. Don't wait for things to happen. If they don't happen automatically, build a fire under them and see that it happens.

I know people who have come all the way through life going the extra mile and wound up in the poor house. They had made two mistakes: they were absolutely honest, which gave everybody a chance to exploit them, and they went the extra mile and became draft horses. I am advocating that you don't become a draft horse. See to it that this law of increasing returns begins to work for you. If you don't watch out, you will find a lot of people who will take advantage of you. I don't tolerate any imposition. I do my part and then see to it that the other fellow does his part. The first law of nature is self-preservation. "Be true unto thine own self," said the great Shakespeare. Be true to yourself; and when you are rendering service that is good in quality, good in quantity, and in the right attitude, make sure that it doesn't fall on barren ground. See that those seeds germinate and grow and yield 100 seeds for each one you put in the ground. See that life compensates you. If it doesn't come from one direction, try another; maybe you will have better luck. If you are working for an employer and giving superior quality and he doesn't recognize that, then begin to look around for another employer.

Number eight: Going the extra mile tends to develop a keen, alert imagination. It is a habit which keeps one continually seeking new and more efficient ways of rendering useful service. It alerts the mind. That alone would justify it.

Nine: It develops the important factor of personal initiative, which gets you in the habit of doing the thing that is expedient. It alerts the imagination so that the imagination recognizes what is expedient. You see opportunities you never saw before. Just think what a difference it is having your mind alerted to opportunity rather than having your mind alerted to recognize alibis or excuses for why you didn't do the thing you should have done.

Ten: Going the extra mile serves to give you better confidence in yourself and puts you on a better basis with your own consciousness.

Eleven: It serves also to build the confidence of others in one's integrity and general ability.

Twelve: Going the extra mile aids one in mastering the destructive habit of procrastination. Did you ever hear of that word? I expect you indulge in that now and then, don't you? Don't we all? This morning when I woke up—I had a very heavy day yesterday and a heavy lecture the night before—and I knew I had a heavy day ahead of me, but I procrastinated about another hour. But do you know that oftentimes that extra hour in the morning, if you don't watch yourself, you will get into the habit, and it will cost you a lot? You have to remember to be on your toes all the time.

When you have the habit of going the extra mile, you are so eager to get that thing done that you love the thing you are doing and the people you are doing it for, and pretty soon that habit of procrastination just dies of starvation.

Thirteen: Going the extra mile helps you develop definiteness of purpose, without which you cannot hope for success. It gives you definiteness of purpose because you are moving and speaking and acting according to motive. Most people move because they have to. They eat and sleep and hold down a job, but they don't really move with definiteness of purpose at all. They just move to keep on living.

Then the QQMA Formula. I want to call your attention to this formula. It means the quality of service you render, plus the quantity of service you render, plus the mental attitude in which you render it fixes the compensation you get out of life. QQMA equals compensation. When I use the word *compensation*, I use that to include all the things that you want in life—money and all the other things. It wouldn't be a bad idea for some of my students to organize themselves into a QQMA club and wear pins to remind themselves that they will get out of life according to the QQ and MA in which they render service.

QQMA Formula
Quality of Service + Quantity of Service + Mental Attitude = Compensation

I want to tell you that if you take away the spirit of this principle tonight as I have sincerely endeavored to transfer it, this may become the most important evening in your life, because it will mark a change in your attitude that will put you on the winning side of the river of life. This is the one thing whereby people can switch themselves from the failure side of life over to the success side of life, and I hope with all my heart and soul that not one person will overlook my sincere attempt to put over to you the mental attitude for carrying out this principle.

CHAPTER FOUR

Applied Faith

June 11, 1947

Everyone who is happy, please hold up their hands. Everybody who is unhappy?

Those of you who are unhappy, you might as well unbutton your coat and loosen your tie now, because you are going to get rid of that unhappiness before the evening is over.

Before we start on the subject tonight, which is Applied Faith, I want to tell you a few things that Applied Faith is not. It is just as well to know both the positive and negative side of this subject, and I am going to give you an illustration by telling you about a very wealthy friend of mine who lives down in Atlanta, Georgia, by the name of Woodruff. He owns a majority of the stock in the Coca-Cola Company, worth between $50 and $75 million dollars. Mr. Woodruff is way up in years, and every time I go to Atlanta, I go in for a visit with him, merely to hear him talk, because he is the most confirmed pessimist I have ever known in my life to have that much money.

The last time I was in to see him, which was about five years ago, he said to me, "I always enjoy seeing you come because you are one of those confirmed optimists who always leaves a little of your optimism with me, although I don't know where you put it." We talked on for a while, and I asked him what his troubles were at this time. And he said, "I am afraid I'm going to die in the poor house." And I said, "Mr. Woodruff, you will never die in the poor house, but you will die poor, you may be sure of that, because you have lost your capacity for riches in the real sense. And this money that is burdening you is not developing faith; it is developing fear. Your major trouble today is that you are afraid you are going to lose this money, and it is wrecking your life."

Then I shook hands with him and walked to the office door and started out, and he yelled at me and said, "Come back here. I want to ask you something. Suppose you were in my place today—suppose you stood in my shoes and had my wealth and money and were about to lose it—what would you do?" I said, "Mr. Woodruff, I have been waiting for you to ask me that question for four or five years, and you are going to really get an answer. Mr. Woodruff, do you really and truly want to know what I would do if I were in your shoes?" He said, "Yes." I said, "Do you want it in the raw?" He said, "That's just the way I want it," and I said, "That is the way you are going to get it." I said, "Mr. Woodruff, the first thing I would do is to take all the interest you have in

Coca-Cola stock and transfer it into United States Government bonds, and then I would go out in the public square and get the police to rope off 50 square feet; and then I would set them afire and burn them up." And he said, "I asked you to be serious," and I said, "I am. I would be sure that my money would go for the benefit of the people of the United States, and I would never again have the fear I would lose my money because I wouldn't have any to lose."

I don't need to tell you that he didn't act on my suggestion. I hardly need to tell you that he is still a wealthy man, getting old and weak and more and more afraid all the time. I needn't tell you that he is giving himself such severe punishment with his burden that I wouldn't undergo it if you gave me the world with all the air around it. Nothing would be worth that price.

There are a lot of wealthy people in the world, not all of them Mr. Woodruffs. Some deal in small weaknesses which are destroying their capacity for faith by worrying that they may lose something. If you really and truly have a fear you are going to lose something, it is better to give it away. Get rid of anything at all that occupies your mind with fear. It is a miserable condition. Find out the cause of the fear and get rid of it at any price. You know the major reason why most people don't use the great capacity of faith? I'll tell you why they don't: they don't have the courage to let loose some of the things they are afraid they are going to lose.

> *If you have a fear you are going to lose something, it is better to give it away.*

I had a large estate before the Depression began—600 acres. There was a 16-acre lake on it. Our house had 40 rooms, all filled. I thought that was smart in the beginning. I found out later it wasn't. I owned another residence once with 16 rooms in it. One night I came home and not a room in the house was empty. There was a man in my bed, and he had on my pajamas—one of my students. I went out and slept in my car. Look what I was trading for what I thought to be opulence.

Then the Depression came along and cut off my income, and I held on to that estate by the skin of my teeth for about two years. And then I wondered why it hadn't occurred to me before that I could just turn it back to the man I bought it from and let him worry about it, and that's exactly what I did. He still has it and is still worrying about it and still paying taxes on it, and I don't have to think about it anymore.

It may seem inconsistent on my part to talk to you about success and then talk about disgorging and dislodging yourself, but there is such a thing as holding onto things that cost you too much in the way of fear and worry, and not all are money either. They destroy the capacity of faith. You know, you can't exercise the pure, clean power of faith, which is nothing more than Infinite Intelligence expressing itself in our lives, as long as there is one iota of fear and worry in your mind about anything. You have to learn to give your mind a mental physic and no matter what the price is, go through with it. That's the first step in conditioning your mind for faith. Get rid of those things that are causing you to be afraid.

These are the basic fears you have to master:

One: The fear of poverty. I have a lot of students in this class who are not getting as much out of this course as they should get, as they would get, if they were not afraid they are not going to have money enough to carry out certain business and professional projects they have in mind. Before I get through with you, you are going to know beyond a question of doubt that the first step you are going to have to take to attain success, economic or financial success, is to get rid of that fear of poverty.

I am going to tip you off to something that perhaps you don't know. You are living in the richest country in the world, the freest country in the world; you are living in the country of the greatest opportunity in the world. You are, perhaps every one of you, citizens of that great country. You live in a country where everything that you can possibly need is available to you at the right time and under the right set of circumstances. Remember, there is no use to be afraid. You get yourself ready for a thing, and it will put in its appearance. Everything does, whenever you are ready for it. You are not going to be ready for financial success, prosperity, as long as you fear poverty, and I am going to give you the instructions to get rid of that before I am through.

The second basic fear that you must kill off is the fear of ill health. The first thing you do is develop a health consciousness. Think in terms of health. Don't imagine you are going to suffer with all the diseases mentioned in the patent medicine ads. They are designed to make you feel sick. If you are listening to Alka Seltzer-sponsored programs every night, which I do, be sure to turn off the commercial as quick as it comes on. It may make a hypochondriac out of you, and that's a bad thing.

How many of you have ever had a little garden of your own? A lot of you who have had the rich experience of raising those marvelous vegetables and flowers that grow out of the garden know there are a lot of things you have to do, and some are not too pleasant. You have to kill off the enemies of those vegetables. The worst enemy is a great crop of weeds that grow a little faster than the vegetables. You have to do whatever is necessary then to cut them out, otherwise those vegetables are going to be wasted. Then you have to water and fertilize the vegetables. That is the same thing you have to do in your cranium. It will grow a rich crop, but you have to keep your mind seeded with the things you want, with faith, and root out those weeds of fear, of doubt, and self-limitation.

There are two kinds of fears: one you can do something about; the other you can't do anything about whatsoever—and get that fear out of your mind, because there is nothing you can do about it. It is beyond your control. Most people don't follow the rule, but instead they worry about the things they can do something about and the things they can't do anything about whatsoever; and in addition to that, they anticipate what might happen and worry about that, too. A lot of things might happen. Almost anything could happen; but if you keep your mind fixed on those negative things that might happen, you may be sure you are not going to be disappointed.

Get your mind conditioned for the expectation of faith. I know of no greater form of faith than that of choosing a definite purpose and keeping your mind so thoroughly filled with desire and the attainment of that purpose that fear has no power to get in. Fix your mind upon some definite thing that you wish to attain, and let that become an obsession with you.

Will you look up that word obsession in the dictionary? Not that you don't know in a general way what it means, but look it up and remember this: just an ordinary wish or hope is not enough to move you; you must have a burning desire for a definite, specific thing. You must have a definite, specific time set within which you are going to acquire this. You can't just say that "in the future sometime, I am going to get hold of enough money to see me through my old age."

There is another fear I want to call to your attention: the fear of criticism. Make up your mind that the next time somebody criticizes you, instead of getting mad or your feelings hurt, you are going to reaffirm and reexamine yourself and make up your mind whether you are right or wrong. And after you do that, you are really going to thank that person for criticizing you, because he probably pushed you one step higher than what you were doing previously.

Don't let people talk you out of what you are doing or let the fear of criticism stop you. Most people say, "I fear what they will say." Who are "they"? "They" are an imaginary group of people that you think might possibly criticize you. Make up your mind what you are going to do. Sell yourself that it is right and then go straight toward the road. Don't look to the right or left. Don't pay attention to criticism or commendation. It is just as wrong to dwell on commendation as it is to take to heart criticism. Start learning to depend on yourself and not to be scared off or impressed by what people might say.

Fourth: fear of the loss of love. My, oh my, what damage is caused because of the fear of the loss of love. It is perfectly useless to fear it. If you lose it, there is nothing you can do about it anyhow, correct? Lots of people are suffering from frustrated love. They have loved somebody who didn't reciprocate or was not worthy. At this point of frustration, you are standing next to the gate that enters into the temple of genius with the key in your hand, if you will only learn to transmute that into some great effort. Put it back of your definite purpose in life, and instead of enjoying the reciprocation of the one you love, express that in something else, like art; create something beautiful; or express it in your business or profession. Turn your attention on that. That is what you can do in the face of lost love.

The greatest man, in my opinion, who ever served as president of the United States was a nobody from nowhere. Born in a one-room cabin in Kentucky, he had practically no schooling. He failed in everything he went into. He went into surveying, and the sheriff seized and sold his instruments. He went into store keeping, and the sheriff seized and sold out the store. He tried the practice of law and won little success in that. He joined the Army and went ahead as captain. In three months' time, they demoted him to a private, and he was lucky he wasn't kicked out of the Army. Then a great tragedy entered into his life. He lost in death the love of the only woman he had ever loved, Ann Rutledge. And that frustration reached very deeply into his soul, and Abraham Lincoln came out of it with the mark of a genius stamped on him. He found the great man that was within him, the great man that is within all of us. All of you have potentialities of greatness, and it often takes some great tragedy to bring this out. Abraham Lincoln, as we know him today, was the result of the transmutation of love.

Now do you see what I mean? Death can bring heartbreak. It is also the nature of people sometimes not to reciprocate. It is the nature of people not to be worthy of love, sometimes, but you don't have to go down under it. You can take the experience and transmute it into efforts that will enable you to accomplish things that you could accomplish in no other way in this world.

So much for the fear of the loss of love. If you have experienced the loss of love of someone, or of money, or of an automobile or a calf or a horse, just remember that you can go back and take up that frustration and fear and transmute it into something very great. Nothing is ever lost in this universe—not even the negative things. You can transmute every adversity into an equivalent benefit.

> *You can transmute every adversity into an equivalent benefit.*

Next, the fear of the loss of liberty. You have to get rid of your fears on that score. To be afraid of the loss of liberty in a great country like ours! No, there is going to be no loss of liberty except insofar as you give your fear room in your temple.

The next one is the fear of old age. I want to say that I feel greatly complimented that there are so many middle-aged men and women in this class. It used to be that people about middle age would commence to have this awful fear. I want you, a lot of other people want you, and there are millions in industry who want you, if you learn to tell them about this philosophy. You are not too old unless you accept this old age fear. Perish the idea that you are too old to succeed in life. You might be too old to dig ditches, but you are not taking this course to do that. You are taking this course in order to release your mind and direct it to higher stations than you hoped to attain in the past.

Let's rededicate ourselves to that purpose tonight. I am speaking not only as the teacher but as a student, because I am rededicating myself to a higher standard; and I am going to attain it, and you are going to help me.

Do you know that when I was building this philosophy, I found that hardly any outstanding man had begun to reach his stride until he had gone well beyond the age of 40, and some of the biggest achievements of men in all walks of life came when they were between 50 and 65—and sometimes much older. The trouble with some people is that they have heard other people all around them expressing fear, and they have seen a lot of people in different businesses fired by employers because of their age. If you are in a business where your age counts against you instead of counting for you because of the accumulated wisdom that age brings, you are in the wrong place. You have nothing to fear if you are beyond the conventional age of 40. I hope the majority of the readers of my philosophy will be beyond 50. I have one student who is almost 80, and I know he will make a swell teacher. He may not live as long, but he will make a swell teacher while he does live.

Next is the fear of death. That comes under the classification of fears you can do nothing about. You can't do anything about death except condition yourself, just as I conditioned myself for dentures. I never think about that except when I am counseling people not to let it worry them. I don't care what happens. I am doing the best job I can on this side of the plane, and when I get on the other side, I won't have any control over it anyway. Do something about that end of life that you control now.

Wouldn't it be awful if you couldn't die? Think of old man Woodruff in bed now, gone to bed finally. Think of the awful thing of having to lie in bed the rest of your life, worrying about the loss of your money. Wouldn't that be a greater ill than anything the orthodox preachers tell you about? Nature has a plan, undoubtedly, and you have nothing to fear from anything that Nature plans. There is no purpose in fearing anything. The only thing is if there is something wrong inside of your life—something that needs healing—it is your job to find out what that is and take care of it.

Now we come to the description of what you must do step by step in the developing of the most important thing in the world, and what would you say that most important thing is? You tell me. Belief in yourself. That's right. Now you have hit the nail right square on the head. Where in the world could you direct faith that would be more beneficial to you than to develop absolute invincible, irresistible confidence, but in yourself? That's the greatest thing you can do with applied faith. If you have the proper amount of confidence in yourself, you can always draw upon the power of faith.

First, you adopt and carry out a definite major purpose in life. You won't probably attain it immediately, but you will start by using the instructions laid down previously. That doesn't mean adopting only an overall, major purpose and that you can't have many minor purposes as well. The biggest thing that you hope to accomplish in your whole life should be your major purpose. And begin associating as many people as soon as possible with you in the Master Mind principle in carrying out this philosophy. If it is nobody but a member of your family, your wife, your husband, some friend, some business associate, find somebody as quickly as you possibly can to enter into the spirit with you, and begin, even in the humblest way, to help to carry out your definite major purpose.

Second, associate as many of the basic motives as possible: your desire for money, your desire to please someone you love, your desire for personal achievement, freedom of body and mind, and whatever other of the basic motives that you can logically place behind your objective. Give yourself a motive for doing what you want to do—a strong motive—and then bring that motive up in your mind at least a dozen times a day and see these things already carried out. If one of the motives is to accumulate sufficient money to give you a fine house, a nice automobile, and a nice wardrobe, you should see all of those things in your mind. If it's a mink coat you want, go into the closet and dust off the mink coat once in a while, and you will soon get that, instead of the old cloth coat. But keep your eyes shut so you won't see the old cloth coat, and sooner or later that old cloth coat will turn to mink. You can make it turn to mink if you see it in your mind's eye.

Connected with your definite major purpose there should be, of course, a stipulation about the exact amount of money that you need the rest of your life—not the amount you expect to get in one lump but will get from month to month and from year to year—and don't compromise for less. Don't pay any attention to that fellow on your shoulder that will clutch onto you and try to put fear into you. Get rid of him. All your fears and doubts, get rid of them.

Next, write out a detailed list of the advantages of your definite major purpose, and call these into mind many times a day, thereby making your mind success conscious. Write out every benefit that you can think of that would accrue to you when your definite major purpose is attained, and think of the joy of working toward it even before you attain it. Benefits will come to you, because when you get your mind in a state of expectancy, it will attract to you automatically many of the things that you want.

> When you get your mind in a state of expectancy, it will attract to you automatically many of the things that you want.

What's the use of using your mind power and your faith if you don't depend upon it? It is like the southern preacher who announced that he was going to pray the following Sunday for rain and he wanted all of the congregation to join in and make up their minds to enter into this prayer because the drought was eating up their cotton. And on Sunday the preacher looked around and saw there wasn't a single umbrella in the place, and he said, "What kind of faith do you call this? We are here to pray for rain, and not one of you even brought an umbrella." I want you to have your umbrellas along. I want you to expect things. I want you to uncross your fingers if you have them crossed, expecting the best in the world of yourself.

If your major purpose is to achieve some material thing or money, always see yourself in possession of it. You know, you can come into the mental possession of money before you come into the physical possession of it. Do you have any conception of what it would mean to you right now if you had a million dollars in the Bank of America? Do you know what it would do to your courage? Do you think it would help you any? Suppose it laid there the rest of your life and you never touched it. Would it be any benefit to you? Oh yes, it would. It would give you the courage to go ahead and do the things you wanted to do, and you probably would make all the money you needed from day to day and from year to year and you would never have to call on that million dollars.

Your subconscious mind doesn't know when you are telling the truth and when you are not. So go ahead and tell your subconscious mind you have a million dollars. If that's too much, say $100,000, but don't settle for less. That's not much now, especially when Uncle Sam gets through chopping it off. I'm trying to give you a modus operandi to get into a state of expectation of the things you want your mind to do. Don't worry about how you are going to do them until you decide that regardless you are going to do everything necessary to carry out your purpose.

Be sure to get into the habit. Make it your business to associate with people who are in sympathy with you, and lead them to encourage you in every way possible. This has reference to close friends or members of your Master Mind alliance only. Don't disclose your purpose to others, most of all not to your relatives. You can see the reason for that. You are undergoing a transformation in your mental attitude; and if you go back and tell those relatives who still have the fear complex that instead of making $6,000, or $7,000, or $10,000, you are jumping to $25,000 next year, they are going to have you examined. Just don't tell them; just go ahead and do it.

Relatives are the worst offenders in the world in this. They are always throwing cold water on you. Don't give them a chance to throw a wet blanket around you if you can possibly avoid it. I don't know of any circumstances where you couldn't keep a relative from going into your mind. It's one place where you have privacy. You can build your purpose in your mind, and you won't have to explain it to your relatives or neighbors or anyone else except those helping you to carry it out.

Next, let not a single day pass without making some kind of physical action to carry out your major purpose. Make some move every day toward the attainment of your major purpose; and if it is not the main one, then carry out one of your minor purposes. In building a brick home, they bring the bricks up, and first they make the foundation and then they mix the mortar and put the bricks in one at a time. It is a highly organized structure and a very strong one and very beautiful, very attractive. And your major purpose in life oftentimes means building a brick at a time, but you have these minor purposes, and be sure you carry out some of them.

Here's another vital thing: choose some prosperous, self-reliant person who is obviously successful as your pacemaker, and make up your mind not only to catch up to that person, but to excel him, and do this silently without mentioning your plans to anyone. This will be vital to your success in a great many instances.

Next, choose and surround yourself with books, pictures, wall mottos, and other suggestive evidence of self-reliance as it has been expressed by others. Build an emotion of achievement. You will see in the offices of great leaders that almost always they have surrounded themselves with an association related to their major purpose in life. You go into a great author's place of business, and the chances are you will see a picture of a great literary man. His shelf will be filled with books of the type he likes best; and even though he seldom reads them, they are there and are part of the emotion. Chances are if you go into a successful businessman's office, you will find almost always that the walls are covered with mottos and pictures of other outstanding men in business. In other words, give yourself physical evidence of things that are related to what you want to be in life. That is called autosuggestion.

Build an emotion of achievement.

There are many of you who know of the job I performed for Robert G. LeTourneau Company of Georgia. I was there one and a half years and did such a successful job that they have no labor problems and never will. They can't have, for management and labor are working too closely together, based upon this philosophy. And I want to tell you one of the most effective things I did there: I wrote hundreds of different mottos, and every day we changed the mottos throughout the factory—a new motto every day of the week—and then we published some of them in book form and gave a copy to every employee of the LeTourneau Company. I had a letter from one of the officials the other day who said, "Now, almost four years since you left our place, the statement that stands out in the mind of every person here and the statement they talk about most is the principle of Going the Extra Mile," and that was the thing I stressed most.

In other words, I plastered that plant and the cafeteria where they would stand in line to get their meals with a statement of this philosophy of one kind or another, such as "remember that your only limitation is the one you set up in your own mind" and "remember that your real boss is the man who walks around under your hat." I was standing in the cafeteria when this last motto was put up, and one man let out a yell and said, "That man Hill knows his onions. I have known all my life that my foreman was a louse." Of course, he didn't mean that, but it shows you what the reactions of different minds will be to a clear statement of English.

Adopt the policy of never running away from disagreeable circumstances. Fight it out with yourself in connection with all such circumstances right where you stand, and do it today before those circumstances get the best of you. Give no thought whatsoever to procrastination. If you asked me to mention the most disabling weakness of mankind as a whole, I would say without hesitation: procrastination. It is the thing that keeps most people from working out a definite purpose in life. It is the thing that keeps most people from carrying it through when they do start it. Get it out of your consciousness. You will then recognize the truth that everything has a definite price, and there is no such thing as something for nothing. The price of self-reliance is eternal vigilance in carrying out the instructions I am about to give you. Your watch word must be persistence.

I learned from a wild crow a great lesson of persistence. I tried to tame this crow. I got him away from the nest, and his mother found out where I took him and told him not to associate with men under any circumstances and never to weaken.

After I had him for a month, he would peck my hand that had the food in it. He would say, "Doggone you, I'm sorry I can't peck your hand off." He didn't really say that, but that's what he meant, and he would walk around and around that pen thousands of times a day. He actually wore his feet down and got corns on them. Finally, my conscience got the best of me. I saw he wasn't going to give in. His mother or father was sitting up in the tree watching him like I am going to watch you to see you don't give in. Finally, I said, "This is cruel because he is never going to be a friend of mine," so I opened the door. And he walked by and looked at it as if he didn't believe it, and he said, "No, it couldn't be, even if I do see it." He would pass that door, and he would say, "No, it can't be true. It's an illusion. It is a trap. He's fooling me." I watched him go around perhaps 100 times, and I went in the house finally and said, "Maybe in the dark he'll stumble into that space."

I never in all my experience saw such a demonstration as to what the law of Cosmic Habit Force could do. He had gone by that place so many times that he knew there couldn't be a door there, but that night he got out. And the old mother crow sure gave me a cussing, but she got her baby back; and that's the last I ever saw of him, but not the last I thought of him. I think of him every day. I wish I could impart to my students one-tenth of that persistence.

Why don't you decide you are going to carry this out, each and every one of you, decide your own time when to start; but if

Applied Faith

it falls short, then start again and keep right on keeping on. Persistence is a marvelous thing; and when you get your mind conditioned to accept the defeats and the experiences that come along to test you, you will find success will come along so fast and so quick you will wonder why you didn't get into this long ago.

There are so many people who could succeed if they had just enough faith. The majority of you are selling yourselves short all the time because you haven't learned the power to awaken and automatically turn on faith. The suggestions I have given you tonight are all you need to turn on the capacity of faith.

There is one story I like to tell my students because it is so significant, so illustrative, of what you will need. One of Sam Jones's children came to him one day and said, "Father, you talk a great deal about God. You know a great deal about God, don't you?" Then he said, "Father, I want to ask you, tell me who made God?" And Sam said, "I have the answer, but you don't have anything to put it in." I'm not suggesting that you don't have anything to put it in. That's not my implication, but that's the inference you make most of the time. You don't recognize that you have something to put it in. You have the ability to come down here and sit two hours, and you can turn on that faith, call into being anything you choose to, and be just as successful in your field as Henry Ford was in his, as Thomas A. Edison was in his, and as Napoleon Hill is in his.

CHAPTER FIVE

Self-Discipline

June 18, 1947

It has been said by psychologists who have studied the subject long and well that man is ruled mainly by his emotions, not by his reason. Not so for the well-disciplined mind, however. The disciplined man balances his reason and his emotions. In other words, what his heart tells him to do he submits to his head, and they strike an agreement. The business of balancing the head and the heart is important. If you learn nothing from this lesson but that, so that your will will have a part in your judgment and your actions, then the time you spend tonight might well become the most important time you have spent up to that time.

The five senses of sight, sound, smell, taste, and touch become reliable only through strict self-discipline. For example, I can close your second and first fingers like that, and place a marble in your hand, and press the fingers down on the marble; and the sense of touch will tell you there are two marbles, and the sense of sight will tell you there is one, and your fingers wouldn't be telling you the truth. Each one picks up its own independent message to the brain, and the brain says there are two marbles.

I could uncork a bottle of plain water, shake some on my handkerchief, make an ugly face, and ask you to raise your hand the minute you smelled that oil of peppermint, and practically two-thirds of you would smell oil of peppermint when there is nothing in the bottle but water. Your sense of smell is not reliable, your sense of touch is not reliable, and you have to discipline them at all times; and even then, you can't fully depend upon them.

The faculty of the memory is the storehouse of all sense impressions. It is the filing cabinet of the mind. It has every impression that ever went into your conscious mind and every impression that ever reached you through your subconscious mind. You may or may not know that a great many things are stored there that didn't go through the conscious section at all. As a matter of fact, some of the most important lessons I have delivered, and some of the most important cures I have effected, were while the client was asleep. My own son, Blair, for instance, you have heard me tell or have read about the method by which I dealt with him, entirely while he was asleep, dealing with the subconscious mind and giving him directions, and he learned from it.

Self-Discipline

Here are the factors of the mind that you can discipline. Number one: willpower or the ego. The ego is the major portion of all there is of you that is of value. The rest of you is a collection of chemicals worth about $0.84 or $0.85 usually, but about $1.85 now with the ego. If they ground you up and separated you into those various chemicals, they wouldn't bring over $1.85, but that part that can't be ground up, which represents the ego, which you must control and discipline, may represent anything from poverty and ill health and sickness on up to anything you envision as your portion in life. In other words, you set the value on your ego.

You set the value on your own ego.

How can you do that? The first step is to discipline it and put it under your direction so it doesn't rule you and instead you rule it. An ego is a powerful thing. Some egos are too weak and too lacking in courage, and some are overdeveloped. I expect you have seen the latter type. One is just as bad as the other. There is a halfway point at which you must arrive in the feeding and encouraging of your ego, but I would say that the average ego on the whole needs feeding more than it does disciplining so that you will have sufficient courage to take possession of your own mind, lay out your own plans, and determine you are going to make life pay off on your own terms.

I recently sat for one hour on my porch talking to one of the students here in this class tonight. He had been making $18,000 to $20,000 a year in the ice cream business in the east. And then something went wrong, and he came out here to the coast; and he is now driving a taxicab, making $35 a week. What do you suppose I said to him? I am not looking in his direction because I wouldn't want him to shift and get red in the face and then you would know who I am talking about. What happened to him? I tried to get him to tell me, and he didn't know; but I did. He had underfed his ego. He had allowed somebody to tramp on his ego, otherwise he would never in the world have consented to drive a taxicab. It is just not profitable enough for a man who has been making $18,000 to $20,000 a year. His ego needs feeding, needs building up, and he is getting it in this class, the kind of building he needs. I didn't charge him, and he can pay me when he makes the first $100,000.

The next faculty that you control when you have complete discipline is the faculty of the emotions. Ordinarily this is referred to as "the heart," where the emotions of love, hate, anger, envy, and greed are. All those emotions come under that heading and must be disciplined.

As a matter of fact, I now want to give you a formula which, if you will get the full significance and apply it, make use of it, it may well become worth ten times as much as you have put into this course. That is, in dealing with your ego, you should regard it as a very precious possession. You should protect it as carefully as you would protect some very fine diamonds if you had them. You certainly wouldn't let them lay around for anyone to look over, but most people leave their ego wide open for anyone to come in and pollute it with thoughts of fear and worry. I am going to give you a system that will make that impossible.

I found out a great many years ago that I would have to do something about this. I drew three imaginary rings around myself. One is a very wide circle, and anybody who has any legitimate business with me, and maybe some who don't have legitimate business with me, can jump over that ring and maybe get some of my help, some of my money. However, there is another ring or wall drawn still closer to me that is much higher and very difficult to scale. Nobody climbs over that wall save only those who have something I want or have something in common with me. I want you to get the significance of that. Don't be too quick to jump to the conclusion that I am mercenary. You can call it whatever you want. I'm telling you how to protect your ego, and it's a necessary thing to do. Those who have legitimate business with me and can establish that we have something in common, a medium of exchange—they have something I need—they can get over that wall, but there they stop.

I have a third wall very close to me and very high, as high as the sky. No human being in my entire life has ever gone over that wall and ever will go over that wall, I hope. So, you can think that over, too. That is where the real ego of Napoleon Hill stays and protects itself. I protect that. In other words, when somebody comes to me with a tale of worry or woe or fear, I never let him get within my ego or over that higher inner wall. I want some of you to remember that, some of you who are carrying the burdens of all your relatives, of everybody, of all the whole world. I won't even let my own worries get inside of that. My wife Annie Lou herself has never been over that wall. I have seen her peeping around, but she has never gotten over it.

There is a very definite psychological reason for what I have just given you, and I'll give you a clue as to what happens in the average person's mind. It is a wide-open book, and anybody who wants to pick that book up, look through the pages, crumple the pages, can do it. They can almost walk away with the book. Don't let people know your thoughts. A great many people have what I call a "pivotal tongue." It is balanced in the middle. They start it going and then go off and leave it. They tell too much.

You have to learn to protect yourself. Don't let anybody draw you out. Don't disclose to anybody what's in your inner self. I'm going to rest the matter there, but I want you to think about that, because that's an important approach to this subject that we are on tonight—giving yourself directions and not being available in connection with whatever whim people have, whereby they might want to reach you and impose their troubles on you.

Now I want to call your attention to some outstanding people who have done outstanding things through self-discipline and the application of some five additional of these principles that you have been studying. The first one on the list is the most powerful man living in the world today, Mahatma Gandhi. Ordinarily, when you speak of a powerful man, you think of a Henry Ford or an Andrew Carnegie or a John D. Rockefeller or somebody with a lot of money, a lot of property, and a lot of people working for him. Mr. Gandhi doesn't own a house, doesn't have any money, doesn't even have a pair of pants, and yet he is the most powerful man living in this world today and perhaps the most powerful man who ever lived in this world. That's an astounding statement until you get down to analyzing it. His power consists of what? When you stop to consider that over a long period of years, step by step, he has defeated the great British Empire with all its soldiers and all its money, when you stop to consider that he has wrested the freedom of India from that nation, using power they didn't understand or chose to ignore, whatever it is, you recognize that he must have been dealing with a very great power, and that consists of these five things.

They are Definiteness of Purpose, first of all. That's the starting point, and I can image well enough just how definite Gandhi's purpose has been down through these three decades during which I have known him. He knew precisely what he wanted, what was his major determination in life, and was determined nothing would defeat him. It was not selfish, I want you to know that. It was not anything to benefit Mr. Gandhi as an individual. It was something to benefit the whole of the great 400 million people living in India. No wonder he had power. It was not selfish; it was very unselfish.

The second thing he used in developing this unusual power was Applied Faith. In other words, he cleared his mind 100 percent of all doubt that he would eventually get freedom for his people. He didn't think in terms of fear of the great British Empire. He cared nothing for them; but he kept his mind fixed entirely on what he wanted, and that opened the channel of his mind to Infinite Intelligence, which is sometimes referred to as faith.

The third factor was the principle of Going the Extra Mile. Nobody told him to do this. Nobody paid him anything to do it. He is not thinking of it in terms of pay. He not only went the extra mile, my friends, but he has gone the extra million miles. Can't you contrast Mr. Gandhi with some people we know in the United States? They would have gone the extra mile, a million of them, if they could have made a million dollars in the business of going. They would have been selling concessions along the way. They would have been cashing in on that power for their own benefit. That's the common tendency, isn't it? Mr. Gandhi wouldn't capitalize on it. He hasn't been going the extra mile for himself.

The fourth factor—I am breaking down the sources of power of the most powerful man in the world today—is the factor of the Master Mind. He has the greatest Master Mind alliance ever assembled on this earth, at least 200 million minds having a capacity for faith. Those minds are all centered upon one basic thought. Discipline, my friends—that is one of the greatest examples of discipline in this world. There has been no fighting between Mr. Gandhi and his followers. There has been a movement that has carried on as if it were entirely one mind, yet it has been functioning in 200 million minds. It is no wonder they are defeating the British government. It had to be that way. There was nothing in the world that could have defeated that, save only a greater Master Mind than Mr. Gandhi's.

The fifth and last thing Mr. Gandhi has is the power of Self-Discipline. How do you suppose he kept his mind centered on a definite specific purpose? Don't you suppose he had opportunity after opportunity to capitalize on that? Don't you suppose he had temptation after temptation to look out for himself? But no, he had the self-discipline to live the simple life. He had no intention of accumulating personal property, save only a little goat's milk and a place to sleep on the floor. He didn't even need a house. And here we are running around like chickens with our heads cut off, looking for a house with inner spring beds and combination radio and goodness knows what else, maybe a new automobile, when we could just as well live like Mr. Gandhi does. When we compare our civilization with his, we can easily see what self-discipline is capable of doing for a man or a woman.

We see this again when oftentimes a foreigner will come over here from the other side, and he will start out with next to nothing. One such man started with just a basket—that's all; just a 25-cent basket—and he goes down to the market and buys some bananas and starts peddling bananas. If he sells one, he can eat one during the day. If he doesn't sell one, he can't eat one. By and by, he makes enough to buy a little cart. He starts pushing the cart. He had oranges and grapes and pears. Soon, by and by you find him in a little shack somewhere with a lot of merchandise gathered around him. Next thing you know he has leased a lot and built a building on it. The next thing you know he has bought the lot and has a great thriving business because he had the self-discipline to make what he had fit his needs. You and I wouldn't have paid the price like that, or would we?

I want to tell you, wherever you find a person who is succeeding in a big way you will find a person who has exercised tremendous self-discipline, especially in the beginning stages. There were times in my own experience when I didn't have friends, not even among my relatives, except my stepmother, and I wondered if she wasn't putting on an act. There were times when my enemies said, "He is talking success and doesn't have two nickels to rub together," and the worst part was it was the truth. There was a time when big business paid no attention to Napoleon Hill at all, but ladies and gentlemen, that time has passed. I put in some 20 years of extreme self-discipline. I had to discipline myself to put up with the lack of interest. I had

Self-Discipline

to have sufficient self-interest and self-discipline to carry myself through those lean years.

And no matter who you are, when you first start, you will find you won't do as well at first as you will after you are going for a while. You can't start out with a class like I have at first. The first class I had consisted of six people; and four of them walked out on me, and one of them refused to pay because he said he didn't get his money's worth (and I think he told the truth). You have got to have self-discipline. You have to discipline your tastes and your style of living and make them fit what you have at the present time, until such time as you have more.

I want to call your attention to another case, the Mormon people. They were persecuted maybe more than any other religion in the United States, if not in the whole word. They were literally driven out of their home state of Illinois by other denominations who didn't like their way of living, and then they loaded all their possessions in wagons and went through the wilderness to Utah. Then the government sent soldiers out to Utah to round them up and pester them and persecute them some more. That was about 100 years ago, and they have no hatred or animosity in their hearts. They have worked hard and prospered. And let me tell you something, during the Depression, H. J. Grant, head of the Mormon Church, announced that no matter how long the Depression lasted or how bad it became, not one Mormon would ever be on government relief, and no Mormon ever was.

Now, never mind about this, you Baptists and Presbyterians and Methodists out there in the class. I am not trying to sell you Mormonism. I am talking about a great people who had to undergo a lot of persecution, and they haven't a word to say about it today. I had the privilege of being their guest for three and a half months. I spoke in Mormon colleges throughout the United States. I became well acquainted with them. They are a frugal people, a fine people, and have no animosity in their hearts about what happened 100 years ago. Isn't that something?

Doesn't it take self-discipline to throw that out of their minds, and doesn't it take self-discipline today for you and I to throw out of our minds the resentment, the indifference, the criticism that comes from other people? Doesn't it take a lot of self-discipline to get that out of our consciousness and not have any thought of striking back or of revenge and hate? If you are going to be a big person, a successful person, you will have to get all that out of your mind.

Let's see what made the Mormons great. First of all, they had Definiteness of Purpose, a strong one. They knew precisely what they wanted. And even though they were chased out of the State of Illinois, they made their way through the wilderness, where they set up their tents. The chances were about 50–50 they would all starve to death on the way. If we had such definiteness of purpose to undergo hardships like they did, without resenting it, what a marvelous people we would be.

Self-Discipline

Next, they had Applied Faith, and next used the principle of Going the Extra Mile, and next the Master Mind, and next and last the principle of Self-Discipline. These are the same five principles that Mr. Gandhi used in developing his power.

Ladies and gentlemen, those five principles represent the thinking that makes the Mormon people respected all over the world today and respected by all other religions. Isn't that something to say about a religious faction to which I do not belong myself?

I want to call your attention to an example of self-discipline in reverse gear—these labor movements in the United States today. Try to measure the labor movement and see what you will get. Self-discipline? No! I want to tell you, the weakness in labor unions today is that they want to do a half day's work and collect a full day's pay. They don't want to go the extra mile. They don't even want to go the first mile. Regardless of what President Truman does to the labor bill, you know that labor is in for a trimming, and public opinion is what will do it, because they don't use self-discipline.

I'm hoping and praying—I know that my prayers will be answered and are going to produce results—that I will, sooner or later, come into contact with a wise and smart labor leader who will embrace my philosophy and start teaching it to his union members and selling employers a contract that says every union member will base his efforts on these 17 principles. And when he does that, I can help him sign up in every industry in the United States, and I will.

A number of people in this class probably belong to labor unions. I belong to one myself. I had to before I could get on the air. Think of that. I couldn't even take my own program on the air without belonging to the union—not until I coughed up $50 and $25 more every month. Just how they benefit me I don't know. I had a letter from them the other day asking me to wire President Truman to veto the Taft-Hartley Bill, and I wired him, alright, and said, "I ask you to pass it." I expect there are a great many more members in the unions who would like to say the same thing.

There is nothing wrong with the labor movement. There is something wrong with those in control of it—lack of self-discipline at the top. That's all there is wrong with the labor movement. Take any business that is not getting along and prospering, and generally speaking, you will find lack of self-discipline somewhere, and generally at the top. You fellows who employ others, just remember that—that generally where there is no harmony in an industry or a business, there is a lack of self-discipline among the leaders. Now we will get over these controversial subjects, but I would be no less than negligent in my duty if I didn't point out this outstanding lack of self-discipline.

Just remember, when you begin to succeed and get into the big money, you will need self-discipline far more than you do now. I have seen a lot of people get to the top and then fall to the ground because they didn't use self-discipline. Take the movie people, people who come into fabulous fortunes so fast that they haven't gained self-discipline, and you will see what happens in a great majority of cases. They lose face and sometimes something very much more important than face—character, reputation, health, and everything else—because of lack of self-discipline.

The principle of self-discipline has reference entirely to only one person, and that person is yourself, the only person that you control. You would like to control other people—wouldn't we all—but we have no assurance that we will be able to control anybody or discipline anybody save only ourselves. And the strange thing about this is that once you have learned to use self-discipline, you then put yourself in a position to control others, but not until you have done that. I daresay if Mahatma Gandhi attended as many night parties as you and I have in the past, perhaps drank as many "inspiring drinks" as we have had, that he would have never become the most powerful man in the world today. His power consists in the fact that he took possession of Mahatma Gandhi first of all. He made a fine job of it and learned to live close to Nature.

I sometimes think that one of the greatest tragedies of life is that there are so many delicatessens, so many drug stores, where we can buy so many concoctions that are no good for human health. Civilization has fastened upon us a great many things that we can get along without, a great many habits. Gandhi has thrown off those habits. He lives simply. He is doing the thing he wants to do and seeing the fruition of his efforts, which are coming in the latter part of life. What a great thing that would be for all of us.

Self-discipline—when you really and truly get this principle into your consciousness and commence living by it, you will find out how few things you can get along with in this world, how few things you really need. Had you ever stopped to think that the majority of people in this country, and I suppose in other countries, devote the major portion of their time to getting money they don't need, can't use, and all it does is to bring about the ruination of their descendants? Money can be a great blessing or a great curse.

Let's limit ourselves to our needs in life, adjust ourselves to our needs, and let the other fellow get his needs, too. There are too many people in life who want too much and make it very difficult for the other fellow. That is not a new kind of "ism," but it is the way people are.

I want you to realize there is a way in which you can take possession of your own mind. You can have everything you need, everything you can possibly use, and you don't have to hurt the other fellow. On the contrary, you can reach out a helping hand to help him get all he needs. That's what this philosophy is for—not only to help you, but to help you to help the other fellow. I want to tell you, if you take this philosophy, complete and apply it, the time will come when there won't be anything in the world you want that you don't have. But you will not get hold of it until you start using self-discipline.

Start by using self-discipline at home. That's the best place to begin practice. In our home, I make it my business to deal with Annie Lou as if I loved her, always had loved her, always shall, and as I always want her to love me. We want harmony always, so we carefully watch our dealings with one another. It's essential that we have harmony in our home, and I use self-discipline.

The best place to begin practicing self-discipline is in the home.

It also takes self-discipline between me and my associates. There are times when the rules of business are such that it makes it very convenient to snap at each other, and most people are too ready for that. In my younger days, I used to go around not only with a chip on my shoulder, but a whole block of wood and a sign up there: "I dare you to knock it off." Finally, I took down the sign, and that helped some, but not enough. Finally, I said, "I will have a shoulder that is fully free, where there is no chip to knock off." I stopped expecting people to find fault, and lo and behold, the world around me began to change from one of lack of harmony to one of harmony and cooperation. I changed that world by changing my own mental attitude.

If you want to compel people to come your way or to cooperate with you, what do you do? You do your part first by having the right kind of a mental attitude toward those people, and then you find how quickly they will change their attitude toward you. If you have a member of the family who is out of step with you—your husband, or your wife, or one of your children, or another of your relatives—don't start by arguing, but start by changing your mental attitude. And when you do speak to that person, go out of your way to soften the words.

You can discipline your own mind to impress anybody if you will take the trouble to do it. There was a fellow who came out to my house when I lived in Florida. As a matter of fact, he came more than 1,000 miles to see me. He came down there to cheat me out of a large sum of money. He had a very well-designed plan, and up to a certain point it worked beautifully. He started out by telling me that of all the men in the world, he envied me most because of my influence and ability to write books. And he said, "I have watched you a great number of years and seen you take possession of an audience for two and a half hours," and you see he was getting pretty close to that circle I have around myself. Then he said, "You know, Dr. Hill, you are overlooking a marvelous opportunity and kind of letting Andrew Carnegie down. Instead of retiring and coming down here to play, you ought to get back into harness and help to cure this world, and you have the only philosophy that can do it."

That gave me a shock, and then came the payoff. He had a scheme whereby if I would only pay him $25,000, he would put me on every radio station in the country, and I would be selling not thousands, but millions, of books a month. Well, you know he had me wanting to do it because he had studied me carefully. He had laid his hand on the spot that represents my greatest weakness, and the only thing that kept him from getting away with the deal was that he hadn't established a relationship that built up confidence. In other words, he was a stranger to me. Anybody who would let that happen would deserve to lose his $25,000.

The reason I am telling you this is that it is going to take more self-discipline when people are complimenting you than when they are condemning you, because flattery is the weakness that has been used to influence people from the dawn of civilization.

There was a man who wrote a book, or rather it was written for him. The central theme is if you want to influence people, flatter them. And they made a million dollars from this book, and when I came out with *How to Sell your Way Through Life*, I devoted many chapters to denying that central theme of that book. It is one of the most dangerous things in the world. It takes a lot of self-discipline not to succumb to flattery.

Remember, when anyone approaches you with flattery, he either wants something you have or he is sincerely appreciative and wants to give you an honest expression of his appreciation.

I get a lot of appreciation for my work, and I can proudly say that the vast majority of it is honest and sincere. But once in a while, a man comes along like I described, and did I not have this philosophy to live by, I might be taken in. And that alone is worth ten times the price of this course, because it gives you a perfect test whereby you can distinguish between true and false on anything.

You will need self-discipline. You may have people around you who will discourage you and who will say the plan you have is foolish or beyond your power to carry out. You will find many more people who want to flatter you, I will assure you of that. You will come to the point sooner or later at which you will want to do something bigger and greater than you have ever done before; and when you do, you are going to be discouraged by some of those who know you best, and the way to defeat them is that you must know without a question of doubt that you have the thorough sympathy of those you confide in, or you don't confide in them. Keep your plan to yourself, and let your actions speak for you. "Deeds not words"—that might become the motto of each of you.

This taxicab driver who came to see me has been discouraged in his home, in his neighborhood, in his job, and I said to him, "If you have been in the milk and ice cream business making $18,000 to $20,000 a year once, you can do it again, and don't let anyone stop you from trying. And I can tell you where to get help if your record bears out what you said, and I am sure it does." I sent him away from the house with the feeling that he can not only equal his achievement, but excel it. In other words, I sold him sufficient self-discipline to believe in himself, and that is where you need this self-discipline—stop this business of selling yourselves short.

It may not be in the best of taste for you to overshoot your ability in the way of ambition, but it is a lot better and a lot safer than to undershoot it, and it will do you a lot less harm. If you aim at a very big achievement and only attain a moderate achievement, you will still have attained something of note. If you allow yourself to be held back in the beginning, you have sold yourself short.

Put yourself in the position of a person who has an idea. He has nursed this idea for a long time, perhaps. He has modified it and tried it out. It would be profitable commercially, but he has done nothing with it. Maybe you are that man. Just stop to consider why you haven't done anything with that idea. The reason is that you didn't have enough confidence in your ability to start looking for a Master Mind alliance to help you carry out that idea. I want you to know, each and every one of you, that you are now connected with a source that can help you to carry out any idea you have if you will apply that philosophy.

How many people in this audience have ideas or plans—business, or professional, or otherwise—through which they could make themselves secure the rest of their lives if they had the right amount of Master Mind cooperation to help them put it over? Look at that! And I have no doubt that some of those ideas are very valuable—some not so good and some worth nothing at all—but in the aggregate those ideas will run into millions of dollars if you will only do something about it. Start where you stand. Don't let the fact you don't have all the things you need frighten you.

Have you ever stopped to think about my own personal story? What a dilemma I was in on that fateful day in 1908 when Andrew Carnegie laid in my lap the opportunity to become the author of this philosophy based on the experience of the most successful men in the world. I hardly knew the meaning of philosophy, and there I was with an opportunity like that. You don't have to use very much imagination to recognize I had to have a lot of self-discipline in order to make myself believe I could do what he wanted me to do. And do you know what turned the scales? It occurred to me that if Mr. Carnegie, who had been the most outstanding industrialist in the United States, thought I could do it, that he must have seen something in me which I didn't see in myself. And I was counting on his faith in me, and I want you to do that with me.

I have been in this business for 38 years, the business of looking into the minds of men and women and finding out what made the failures and successes. I wouldn't pretend to know all about it, but I do know a great deal more about it than I did years ago; and it is the rarest thing in the world when a person comes to me and puts himself in my hands that I fail to help that person attain his object in life, if he stands by and doesn't quit.

One of the things that Mr. Carnegie saw in me was the quality of stick-to-it-ness. I didn't have to have the knowledge myself. I knew I could get it from other people. The thing that caused him to turn 250 others was the lack of stickability, and he saw I had that quality. I didn't know I had it, and I am telling you, each and every one of you, that you have to have that quality in taking you from where you are to where you want to go, because otherwise you have been selling yourselves short.

Your success and your failure are entirely a matter of how you make use of your own mind.

If I live to be 100 and you have the privilege of sitting in with me for the next many years, I would never say anything more valuable than I have said in the last five minutes. Each one of you is a potential success now. You have every quality in the world it takes to succeed if you will only use what you have with this philosophy; and in order to do that, you have to use self-discipline. You have to believe in yourself. You have to make demands on yourself, and you have got to forget about other people, so far as influencing you is concerned. It is not your business to influence other people until you have first influenced yourself, and then by persuasion and example and not by force. The best way in the world to impress anybody is to set him a fine example of how you are doing and what you are doing.

This is a very warm evening, and it takes a lot of self-discipline on my part to keep from wanting a drink of water. But I am determined that not one of you is going to get out of this room tonight until you recognize that the most important thing in the world is the power that you have to use your own mind. Nothing has struck me as being so significant as the fact that the Creator considered that the power of the mind is the most important thing, because if you control that, you control everything. Your success and your failure are entirely a matter of how you make use of your own mind.

CHAPTER SIX

Cosmic Habit Force

June 25, 1947

We come now to the last lesson of this particular series, and I believe this is the most profound subject of the entire course, that subject being Cosmic Habit Force. I shall try to give you a clear meaning of Cosmic Habit Force, and then I shall also try to give you a clear description of how you may adapt yourself to the law so as to benefit by it. The purpose of this lesson is to describe the law by which one acquires habits—a law so stupendous in its scope and power that it may be difficult to understand except by those of you who have some knowledge of the sciences.

This law is known as Cosmic Habit Force. It pertains to the universe and the laws which govern it. This is a law by which the equilibrium of the universe is maintained in an orderly manner through established habits. The law forces every living thing to adhere to it, including the physical habits and the thinking habits of mankind. This law forces upon every living creature the dominating influence of its environment. If you let your mind dwell upon poverty and fear, this law takes over that thought pattern, cuts it deeply into the brain cells, and proceeds to direct your life according to that pattern.

The purpose of the Philosophy of American Achievement, on which the previous lessons are based, is to enable one to establish habits that lead to the financial security, health, and peace of mind necessary for happiness. In this lesson, we examine briefly the law in Nature which makes all habits permanent. With the application of this principle, one may set up any desired habit, after which the habit is taken over by Cosmic Habit Force and made to carry on automatically.

Here are some of the habits far removed from human relationships which are governed by Cosmic Habit Force. First of all, the stars and the planets as they are related to one another out there in the heavens are governed by it. Isn't it a marvelous thing to look up into the heavens on a starry night and see all those millions of stars and recognize that those are only a small number of the stars in the universe? They work like clockwork—never collide, roll on eternally to some unknown destiny as the result of a preconceived plan. And no matter what our religious views may be, we recognize and know that Infinite Intelligence is behind that plan. If anyone is in any doubt as to the existence of Infinite Intelligence, that person needs only to study the stars and the planets and the precision with which they are related to one another.

We may also see evidence of Cosmic Habit Force in the seasons of the year as they come and go. We know without doubt that we are going to have certain seasons. They don't always occur in the same intensity or cover the same exact period of time, but they do come and go, year in and year out, because the law of Cosmic Habit Force is arranging and controlling the causes of those seasons.

This law operates in the reproduction and growth of everything that grows from the soil of the earth, causing each seed to produce precisely its own kind without variation and directing the reproduction of every living thing, from the smallest insect and microscopic form of life up to man.

There isn't anything you can imagine that isn't controlled by Cosmic Habit Force. Why, even the electrons and protons of matter maintain a fixed relation to one another and to matter as a whole by a law that so far defies the efforts of man to uncover it. The reactions of matter, from the smallest particle, which is the electron and proton, to the largest stars, are based upon and fixed by the habits of Cosmic Habit Force.

Cosmic Habit Force is the controller of all natural laws. Did you ever stop to think that a great variety of natural laws are operating all the time and that none of them is in conflict with another? They harmonize with one another perfectly. This points to the fact that there must be an overall controlling law, and this controlling law is Cosmic Habit Force.

Napoleon Hill's *Positive Influence*

Incidentally, you may be interested in knowing that before this law of Cosmic Habit Force was revealed to me ten years ago, there was a deficiency in this Philosophy of American Achievement which made it impossible for me to apply it perfectly at all times or to teach others how to do it. In other words, on certain occasions I could make the law of success work, and on other occasions I could not. I found the same thing to be true among my students. After this law was revealed and became a part of this philosophy, the percentage of successes went up, and it is still going higher and higher.

Before I discovered the law of Cosmic Habit Force, my own business affairs ran in cycles of four years. On a graphic chart which I kept, my successes and failures went up and down, making a complete cycle in four years. It would go for one or two years and then start back down. At the end of the fourth year, it was back down to the baseline. A chart of my career indicated that this cycle was repeated from the year of 1908, when I first took the assignment from Mr. Carnegie to organize this philosophy, until 1937. That year I had revealed to me the law of Cosmic Habit Force, and from that time until now my success line has been going up.

This is significant, because if I can make it work for myself, I can teach you to make it work. Our thought habits are automatically fixed and made permanent by Cosmic Habit Force, no matter whether they are negative or positive. Man creates a pattern of thought by repetition of thought on a certain subject, and the law of Cosmic Habit Force takes over these patterns and makes them permanent, unless and until you consciously rearrange them.

Here is the most astounding fact: man is the only living creature equipped with the power of choice by which he may establish his own thought patterns, or break items up and rearrange them at will. You know that every creature on earth below the intelligence of man is fixed and bound by what we call instinct. It has no choice of breaking those habits. Every generation of creatures lower than man comes and goes, taking on the natural process of the preceding generation, and makes no improvement and no changes. Though man is the only one who has the privilege and the right to set his own patterns and to force Cosmic Habit Force to carry them out automatically, only a very small percentage of men make use of this great prerogative.

> *Man is the only living creature equipped with the power of choice by which he may establish his own thought patterns.*

Now let's see how Cosmic Habit Force may be of benefit to one in connection with physical health. I can't think of anything more beneficial to one than a system by which one may maintain perfect, sound physical health. The individual may contribute to the healthful maintenance of his physical body by establishing habit patterns in connection with the following subjects:

First: In connection with the thinking, a positive mind leads to the development of what is known as a "health consciousness," and Cosmic Habit Force carries out that thought pattern to its logical conclusion. But it will just as readily carry out the picture of an ill health consciousness created by the thought habits of the hypochondriac, even to the extent of producing the physical and mental symptoms of any disease on which the individual may fix his thought habits through fear.

It is a fact well known to medical science that the hypochondriac who allows his mind to fix itself on any disease sooner or later develops that disease. I had that brought home to me very strongly by an old lady named Sara Anne Seal when I was growing up in Virginia. She used to come to see my grandmother every Saturday afternoon. She would sit on the front porch and smoke her clay pipe and entertain grandmother with tales of her expected illnesses. She would always place her hand on her left breast and say, "Oh land sakes, I just know I am going to have cancer." I heard her say that a hundred times and wondered what she meant by it. Years passed, and I went away; and my father sent me a copy of a local paper, and on the front page I saw the notice of the death of Sara Anne Seal, who died from cancer of the left breast. In other words, she had thought and talked about it until she finally got it. That is perhaps not a typical example of what happens when the mind begins to fasten itself on the fear of ill health, but certainly cases such as that are not infrequent.

It stands to reason, my friends, that if the mind can and actually does induce the disease of cancer because the mind is focused on that, the mind can and will produce a condition of sound physical health as well. It does not create a negative condition without also being able to create a positive condition to offset that.

Whenever the law of Cosmic Habit Force takes over a thought pattern and carries it out automatically, the thought pattern operates something like a phonograph record. By the repetition of thought on a certain subject, the mind cuts into the brain groove, like the groove on a phonograph record. It can be compared to the needle. That needle goes deeper and deeper until finally Cosmic Habit Force places one in the position of having completed a fixation—that is to say, an idea fixation of thought, either good or bad.

Cosmic Habit Force applied to this business of keeping healthy is obviously of great benefit in connection with the subject of eating. The mental attitude and the thought patterns established while one is eating and during the following two or three hours while the food is being broken down to a liquid form for introduction into the body through the blood may determine whether the food enters the body in a suitable form for the maintenance of sound health. It is a well-established fact that the power of one's thoughts enters into and becomes a vital part of the energy that is carried into the body through the food; accordingly, worry, fear, and all negative thoughts poison the food. Therefore, controlled thought habits during mealtime are of the utmost importance in the maintenance of health. I would no more think of sitting down and eating, my friends, when I was worried or when I am angry than I would think of going to the drug store and getting a bottle of strychnine and taking a good dose of it.

If you want evidence that the emotions and thoughts enter into and become a part of the things you eat, you only have to observe the fact that anyone knows that if a woman who is nursing a baby is worried or has a fear, the baby will have colic in a matter of minutes. In other words, the mother passes on to the baby her thought impulses and fears. The mealtime is, or should be, a period of comfort, and to some people it is an hour when you sit down with pleasant thoughts and pleasant words for those with whom you are dining. Instead of that, the average family uses the mealtime as a mean of punishing the children, disciplining the husband or wife, or washing of family linen (and none of it is clean). You know that this is no exaggeration, and the reason is that the one who has a bone to pick with another member of the family is sure to find that person where he can be reached at the meal hour. The meal hour should be an hour in which you express gratitude, not criticism or anger.

One of the most pleasant periods of my day's work and life consists of rising, when my wife comes into the bedroom with a nice, cold glass of orange juice, and I get up, put my feet in my bedroom slippers, sit on the side of my bed, and say, "Prince of sound health is coming, and down the hatch" and "This wonderful, sweet orange juice which Nature has prepared for me, I want you to take this orange juice and give it to whatever part of my body needs it most, and I am grateful." You will be surprised what a breakfast I can eat after that. It fixes me for the day. It causes my body to receive that orange juice and direct it and make the vitamins out of it because the law of Cosmic Habit Force is operating in connection with my thoughts with the food I put in my stomach.

Just remember the law of Cosmic Habit Force is mixing your thoughts with the food you put into your body. If you do remember that, you will never sit down to eat until you can clear your mind of all worries, fears, and anxieties. I recognize that there are times when you have such anxieties, but at such times it is far better to go without your meal and bide your time until you can sit down with a clear mind than to eat at that time.

And Cosmic Habit Force has a definite connection in relation to one's work, the thing that you devote most of your time to, the source of your income. And here, too, mental attitude becomes a vital ally of the silent repairman that is working on every cell of the body while one is engaged in physical action. Therefore, work should become a religious ceremony with which only positive thoughts are mixed. The famous Mayo Brothers have discovered that four vitally important factors must be observed to maintain sound physical health, and they are as follows: (1) work, (2) play, (3) love, and (4) worship. Those four factors must be balanced one against the other in approximately equal parts or ill health will result. The Mayo Brothers discovered this truth after treating thousands of men and women in their famous clinic. Work must be well mixed with play and worship must be mixed with love or ill health will occur in some form or other.

For comparison, consider the person who has the habit of griping and performs all work grudgingly and in a negative frame of mind. It is a well-known fact that such individuals are seldom physically well but rather they are constantly ailing—some of it real, some imaginary, but all of it destructive of sound health. I can tell you another thing about the griper: about nine out of ten of them, if they are of the confirmed type, have stomach ulcers. And there is only one thing that causes stomach ulcers, and that is an upset state of mind. And there is only one thing that will cure those ulcers, and that's a positive mental attitude. That's worth knowing, isn't it? I have known a great many people who believed that they could cure stomach ulcers by surgical operations. Some of them would temporarily cure such diseases, but the cure was not permanent because there was no change in mental attitude.

For the most part, the major portion of all illness comes about as a result of maladjustment of the human mind. You can make yourself sick with your thoughts or you can make yourself well in most instances. Of course, there are certain chronic conditions where it takes something more than the use of the mind to cure physical ailments. But in the beginning, in the inception, when these ailments were getting a foothold, then you could have eliminated them if you had taken possession of your mind and carried out positive thoughts automatically. In a little while, I shall give you the formula through which you take possession of your mind and place Cosmic Habit Force back of it.

Now we approach a description of the relationship of Cosmic Habit Force to the subject of economic and financial benefits. In case you don't feel impressed by my description of the part that Cosmic Habit Force plays in building and maintaining sound health, I know you will be interested when I begin my description of how you may use Cosmic Habit Force to help you make more money. We start first with the most important principle of this philosophy, which is that of a definite major purpose, which, as you know, is the starting point of all success.

Through a combination of the principles of the Philosophy of American Achievement, one may condition his mind and body to hand over to Cosmic Habit Force the exact picture (through his thought habits) of the financial status he wishes to maintain, and these thoughts will be automatically picked up and carried out to their logical conclusion by an inexorable law of Nature which knows no such reality as failure.

This philosophy is the medium by which one's thought habits may be controlled until they are taken over by Cosmic Habit Force, and it is well to call attention to the fact that no one has ever been known to become financially independent without having first established a prosperity consciousness, just as no one may remain physically well without having first established a health consciousness.

It is a fact well known to psychologists that poverty-stricken people maintain a poverty consciousness, some of them from early childhood on through life. They think in terms of poverty. They fear poverty. They talk poverty. They expect poverty, and that is precisely what they attract to themselves. There must be some power behind it that is responsible.

And now let me call your attention to the proper method of breaking the hold of Cosmic Habit Force on a poverty consciousness and substituting in its place a prosperity consciousness. Here are the instructions for the student who wants to overcome poverty consciousness. They must adopt and carry out a definite major purpose in life. Listen to these instructions carefully, and above all, recognize the relationship between this formula I am now going to give you and the power of Cosmic Habit Force, because Cosmic Health Force is the agent or power or force that makes this formula effective. Here they are.

First of all, write out a complete, clear, and definite statement of your major purpose in life; sign it and commit it to memory; then repeat it orally at least once every day and more often if practical. Repeat it over and over, thus placing back of your purpose all of your faith in Infinite Intelligence. The reason for writing out your definite major purpose and repeating it over and over is to give Cosmic Habit Force a preliminary pattern to follow. The length of time you have to keep conditioning your mind by repetition before you start getting results depends almost entirely on the amount of faith and enthusiasm that you put back of those words expressing them. Those two factors are important, because Cosmic Habit Force works very slowly when you do not express faith and enthusiasm. It works very quickly where faith and enthusiasm are strong.

Next, write out a clear definite plan by which you intend to begin the attainment of the object of your definite major purpose. State the maximum time allowed for the attainment of that purpose, and describe precisely what you intend to give in return for the realization of your purpose. Remember that there is no such reality as something for nothing; that everything has a price which must be paid in advance in one form or another.

The time element is very important. If you say to yourself, for example, "Sometime during my life I want $100,000," Nature will say, "You are uncertain; and if you don't know just exactly when you want it, how you are going to get it, and what you are going to give in return, we will just put it on the waiting list, and maybe you will get around to those important details later on." Most people never do. They have mere hopes or wishes, but Cosmic Habit Force is not impressed by hopes or wishes—especially wishes. A hope can be intensified until it becomes faith, but generally speaking, it is just a glorified wish. We all have many wishes. We wish for wealth, health, maybe a handsome partner in marriage. This philosophy is not based on such wishes. It is a philosophy with precise rules; and if you follow the rules, the results will be just as definite as when you apply the rules of mathematics.

Third, make your plan flexible enough to permit changes at any time you are inspired to do so. Observe that word *inspired*. It means simply that Infinite Intelligence may hand you a better plan than the one you have laid out. Treat such inspiration civilly, because it will help you to strengthen your plan where it is now weak. Understand, you do not change your major purpose. You change only the method of carrying it out. Almost every student whom I have had the privilege of serving personally through counsel has come to me with a weak plan. I often have to change those plans to make them sound. Remember that Infinite Intelligence may present you with a plan far superior to any you can create. Therefore, be ready to recognize and adopt any superior plan which may be presented to your mind.

Fourth, keep your major purpose and your plans for attaining it strictly to yourself except insofar as you have received additional instructions regarding the Master Mind principle.

The reason for keeping this definite major purpose to yourself except for those members of your Master Mind alliance is that the moment you announce to your relatives and friends that you have set a high goal for yourself and give them an idea of the nature of that goal, through lack of confidence in you or envy of you they will start criticizing you and put the seeds of doubt in your mind. Unless you have a very well-disciplined mind, those seeds of doubt will become very insidious. They will germinate and grow and will have just the opposite effect in connection with your definite major purpose. They will have the effect of negating that, and Cosmic Habit Force will further implant these seeds of doubt.

This law of Cosmic Habit Force is absolutely neutral. It feeds upon the fear you give it. If you allow the fear of criticism—any suggestion of doubt—to subdue you, you will be sure not to realize your major purpose. I emphasize this because the majority of people are inclined either to boast or let their enthusiasm run away from them and will speak of their ambitions in the future tense. If you must speak of your ambitions, speak of them in the past tense, not in the future. And speak of them with deeds accomplished and not words, and then nobody can justly criticize you. Nobody can throw a monkey wrench in the machinery or stick out a foot as you go down the pathway of life.

You know, there are people who are not successes themselves and envy other people who are successful, and they would like to stand on the sidelines and wait for the man whose chin is high and slyly stick out a foot and see him go down. Remember this trait of mankind. Just keep your plans to yourself until they materialize into actual achievements. I expect that as long as you live, you will not hear any advice more important to you than the advice you have received in the past ten minutes.

These instructions call for no effort that you may not easily put forth. They make no demand on your abilities which the average person may not comply with, and they are completely in harmony with all true religions.

We come now to the subject of fixations as related to the law of Cosmic Habit Force. First of all, I want to tell you what the word fixation means. To a doctor, for example, it is something to be dreaded, for it connotes a fixed tendency of the mind to cling to the belief that one has a given form of illness, and all such imagined illnesses are most difficult to cure. Fixations occur more frequently in connection with such diseases as cancer, tuberculosis, leprosy, and diabetes. But mental habits become fixed also, such as poverty consciousness and prosperity consciousness—fixed through the law of Cosmic Habit Force.

I am going to give you a list of negative types of habits, which, if allowed to dwell in your mind, will become fixations and will be carried out until such time as an adversity or accident breaks their grip on you, or you deliberately break them through your willpower. These negatives are poverty, imaginary illness, laziness, envy, greed, anger, hatred, jealously, dishonesty, drifting without aim or purpose, irritability of mental attitude in general, vanity, arrogance, cynicism, sadism, and the will to injure others. That is an outstanding list of the major negatives that become fixations in a person's mind and to a large extent wreck one's chances of attaining and maintaining a successful situation in life, because it is obvious that if all these or any of these occupy your mind, the power of faith cannot and will not enter. Every single one of the negatives may become a fixation in your mind, and if you don't get rid of it, you may be sure you will never be able to make 100 percent use of the power of faith.

Now, here comes the positives, and you may want to write out this list and go about deliberately causing every one of these traits to become fixations in your mind. These are the kind you want and that you can work to voluntarily develop.

The first one is definiteness of a major purpose in life. Start your fixation with that point. I just gave you the formula through which you go about carrying out this definite major aim in life, and that same formula is the method by which you translate your definite major purpose in life to a fixation. Automatically, that major purpose is operating to influence your mind, make it more alert, make your imagination more vivid, develop more enthusiasm, give it a greater willpower, and cause you to recognize more opportunities to carry out your definite major purpose as you go along.

Definiteness of a major purpose in life is the first one, then faith. Faith should become a fixation, and the way you make that a fixation is to study the habits opposite to faith, which are fear and doubt and self-imposed limitations, and eradicate those habits. That is to say, don't let your mind dwell on them. Let your mind dwell on beliefs, not disbelief.

Then, personal initiative. That should become a fixation. At first you have to voluntarily engage in personal initiative, doing the thing that has to be done without somebody telling you to do it, moving under your own willpower; but if you do that often enough, it will become a fixation.

Enthusiasm—you should be able to turn it off and on like water in a spigot. And if you ever become a great teacher or a great salesman or merchandiser of your own services, you will have to learn to turn your enthusiasm on and turn it off in order to defend yourself, because there are times if you turn on too much the other fellow will manipulate that to make you do something you don't want to. Make it a fixation subject to change as needed. You may think that is difficult, but it is not. A little practice will enable you to do it. I can turn my enthusiasm off and on just as easily as I can turn on an electric light by pushing a button, and you can, too. There are times when you won't want to turn on all the enthusiasm you can demand because it is contagious, and the other man picks it up and oftentimes hands it back to you as his own.

The next is to go the extra mile, and that is something you can control. And the way to make that a fixation is to start today to do something that you don't expect to be paid for directly. Render some sort of useful service to another person that you do not expect a monetary return for right away. If nothing else, call up that person with whom you have not been on such good terms tonight when you get home, and tell him what a fine lecture you listened to tonight, and tell him you hope he is in the same frame of mind. He may think you have gone crazy, but he will like the attention just as well.

Going the extra mile is a marvelous thing because the law of Cosmic Habit Force grips you and makes that habit permanent so that you no longer go the extra mile for the purpose of getting that person to remember it, but you also go the extra mile because it makes you feel better. When you reach that stage, then the habit of going the extra mile has become a fixation—and a very valuable one, too.

Imagination can become a fixation. The traits of building a pleasing personality can become a fixation. Accurate thinking also becomes a fixation. You know, most people have a fixation in connection with thinking, but it is not connected with accurate thinking but instead in connection with guessing, moving based on the opinions of others—popular opinions that they pick up mostly from the newspapers, or from gossip, or from hearsay evidence. You will recognize when you get into this philosophy there is a way of creating a fixation on the subject of thinking accurately so that whatever you go to do, such as render a judgment or give an opinion, you will do it scientifically and accurately. You will stop this business of having snap judgments. You will also recognize that nobody has any right to an opinion about anything at any time save only the opinion based on study and analysis, data and facts, or what seems to be accurate information.

You have heard me speak many times of the vast majority of people going all the way through life with their minds fixed on all the things they don't want, such as doubt, fear of old age, fear of the loss of love, and poverty, and they get every one of those things they fear. In other words, the mind does attract to it the kind of things it feeds on. And it is up to the individual to feed the mind on what he wants, and the thing that does that is the law of Cosmic Habit Force. Everything one does is the result of habit. Sometimes it is voluntary, and sometimes it is involuntary, such as breathing or the circulation of blood, but all habits are made permanent unless broken by the power of will.

All habits are made permanent unless broken by the power of will.

The way to health, the way to happiness, is by controlled habits. You can make your habits what you wish them to be. All habits that are voluntary begin with the controlling of one's thoughts, and that happens to be the only thing over which the Creator has given man complete control. The very fact that he gave man the right to change these habits is the best evidence that the power of thought is the most important thing in the universe, the most powerful in the whole universe, the thing nearest to Infinite Intelligence, and perhaps actually it is a part of Infinite Intelligence.

You will find that Cosmic Habit Force is the most important of the aspects of your life. The center of it is in the thoughts that you control, and you control the key to those thoughts. You can think in terms of poverty. You can think in the terms of prosperity. Those thoughts are taken over and carried out to their logical conclusion by the most economical natural means. There is nothing supernatural about the way the law of Cosmic Habit Force operates.

The human ego is the most important part of the human being, and I now wish to call your attention to the modus operandi by which you develop, build, and control the human ego, placing the law of Cosmic Habit Force squarely back of your efforts.

First: One must ally himself with one or more persons, and that alliance must be continuous and active. I wish to impress upon your minds that word active. A dormant alliance will avail you nothing. When you work out an alliance with one or more people to help you attain your major purpose or some minor purpose, remember that the law of Cosmic Habit Force goes to work immediately in an active alliance but not where you have merely an understanding but no action.

Second: Under the influence of this association, you must adopt some definite plan by which you attain the objective of that alliance and then proceed to put that plan into action immediately. The plan may be a composite plan by all of the members of the Master Mind group or a plan created by yourself.

Third: You must remove yourself from the range of every person and every circumstance which has even the slightest tendency to cause you to feel inferior. Positive egos do not grow in negative environments. On this point there can be no excuse for not complying, and failure to observe this will ruin your chances of success.

Fourth: One must close the door on any past experiences that have the slightest tendency to make one feel inferior—and that's important, this business of closing the doors on the past. Don't go back and dig up those experiences of the past, of doubt, inferiority, sorrow, or whatever it is. Let the door stay shut—not only close the door, but nail it shut. Don't permit somebody coming along with a skeleton key to try to open it up for you. Nail it fast, and then don't try to open it up with a chisel. Strong, vital egos cannot be developed by dwelling on the past. Vital egos thrive on the hopes and desires of the yet unattained objective. Once in a state of mind of hope, faith, and desire, Cosmic Habit Force goes all out in your behalf to change your hopes and desires into their financial or material equivalent. That's the way the law works.

Fifth: One must surround himself with every possible physical means of impressing his mind with the nature and the purpose of the ego he is developing. For example, the author should set up his shop in a room surrounded by pictures, mottos, and the works of other authors, and he should fill his bookshelves with books related to his own work. He should set up in his own mind that picture which he wishes to express, because that picture is the pattern which the law of Cosmic Habit Force will pick up and transfer into its physical equivalent.

Sixth: The properly developed ego is at all times under the control of the individual. There must be no inflation of the ego in the direction of egomania by which some men destroy themselves.

Let me call your attention to that fact that Nature breaks up established habits of man every so often through war, economic disaster, or epidemics of disease. And when these adversities come along and war or disease breaks up the habits of man, you may look on them as catastrophes, whereas they are actually blessings in disguise. Nature has at all times a definite plan for all things, including this little grain of sand on which we live and the larger bodies in the heavens, and she is not going to tolerate any interference with that plan. All this is a means of preparing you for growth.

It is foolish to speak of "going back to the old things," the old party line in politics. Those days are dead, and let's hope they stay dead. The old orthodox form of fear and superstition of religion is dead too, and Nature is trying to impress a greater thing on the minds of men. And the old slave way of dealing with workers is dead, too, or is definitely dying, because Nature abhors the slave way and is seeing to it that relations by which men try to enslave other men are broken by wars, strikes, and other means.

I think there is no doubt in anybody's mind but that the Second World War got to the point finally where it was out of the hands of any man or any group of men. It was like a brush fire set by one match which then becomes a vast forest fire. In this process of burning things out in war, probably Nature had in mind changing the habits of men and enabling us to start all over with a clean slate with bigger and better things and more just relations to one another, and let's hope that is what the war will bring.

The old way of wars as a means of settling differences between nations is on its way out, too, but not going out so fast as it could, because the majority of people are thinking and talking about the next war. They are literally creating a third world war before the second is paid for, even before it is ended. We couldn't possibly have anything short of a third war if the majority of people are reading scary headlines and thinking about it and talking about it, because consequently Cosmic

Habit Force will take over that scare and bring it to fruition in the form of a third world war. If you want to know the way that wars are made, study the thinking of mankind, and then recognize how the law of Cosmic Habit Force works. Men are afraid. Maybe for all we know it is part of an overall mosaic or plan which Nature is putting into operation, and that which men believe they are doing may be serving some plan beyond our comprehension.

Men of achievement may be parts of an overall mosaic picture, pattern, or plan, and that which they believe they are doing may be actually serving some purpose beyond their comprehension, such men as Thomas A. Edison. He may have believed he was in the business of invention for the purpose of his own financial improvement. Nature may have had another idea, may have wanted Mr. Edison to avail himself of greater improvements for the benefit of mankind.

Henry Ford—every time I think of that man, from the day I first met him, I think how little he had in the way of personality, how little he had in the way of education, and what great achievements he brought forth. I can't help but think that perhaps he, too, may have been a part of this great force of Nature which put herself in harmony with him.

Thomas Paine—that immigrant man who came over here from another country, poor and unknown, did more than all of Washington's soldiers combined, not only to start the Revolution but to educate men to the necessity of fighting for freedom.

One man did that. One man, plus the power of Cosmic Habit Force, put this in the minds of men in such a definite way that they were forced to act upon it.

And Robert Ingersoll—I can't conceive of a great brain like that, perhaps the greatest this generation has ever produced, not having been put here to break up orthodox habits. And Voltaire, and yes, even Joe Stalin. We look upon him as a murderer and a creator of war, which he clearly is. But maybe he is also a creature placed here to break up the habits of men, and Lord knows we could use better habits today.

I want to call your attention to two things which are examples of the way in which we think, and I would refer you to Benjamin Kidd's book called *The Science of Power*. In that book, he calls attention to the two great forces which are working in the minds of men to make us what we are. One is social heredity, and the other is physical heredity. Physical heredity is the law of Nature through which the sum and circumstances of all the characteristics and traits and physical aspects of your ancestors back down through the ages have been handed on to you, and you are part of the sum and substance of all your ancestors. Nature has fixed that for you. And if you come here with a sound physical body, fine. If you come over with a hunchback, it is just too bad, because there is very little or nothing you c3an do to change the appearance of that kind of condition, because the law of physical heredity has fixed that.

But another thing that constitutes what one is is known as social heredity, and it consists in every influence you come in contact with from the time you reach the age of consciousness until death. The newspapers you read, your education, the conversations you hear between other people, the religious influences, the ideas of politics are the result of social heredity, excepting a rare few instances when an individual will break away from this and have thoughts of his own. And when that happens, you will have a Thomas A. Edison, or a Voltaire, or a Henry Ford, or a Paine, or an Ingersoll. The vast majority, however, are victims of social heredity.

I had that brought home to me most forcefully when I was quite a youngster and I was offered this commission by Andrew Carnegie. I was having a luncheon with Senator Taylor, formerly governor of Tennessee, in the Senate dining room. We sat and talked about politics, and I had just received my commission from Andrew Carnegie to become the author of this philosophy. I was enthusiastically telling him about it and how proud I was that I was a southern Democrat and that it was through his influence I got my interview with Andrew Carnegie. He straightened up and said, "By the way, my young friend, speaking of politics, would you mind telling me why you happened to become a Democrat?" I said, "No, I wouldn't mind telling you at all. My father was a Democrat, my grandfather was a Democrat, and my great-grandfather was a Democrat." And he said, "Just what I thought. Wouldn't it have been too bad if your ancestors had been Republicans?" I became very angry at the time, but afterwards it caused me to do some real, logical thinking. And I can safely say this: from that day to this, I have never been anything, thought anything, or done anything just because somebody else did. I had to have my own individual reason, and that was the beginning of real growth in my way of thinking.

When you break away from those influences, break away from social heredity, from what your mother or father thought, and do your own thinking, that's a great day in your life, no matter who you are. Social heredity is under the direction of the law of Cosmic Habit Force.

Now let me call your attention to one case where the law of physical heredity was made to correct its mistake and the law of Cosmic Habit Force was brought into play to make Nature correct her mistakes, and that was in the case of my second son, Blair. Many of you remember having heard me relate this story, and all of you who read *Think and Grow Rich* know it; but let me call your attention to the significance of that. It began when my child was born without a sign of ears—no cavity to the skull, no equipment of hearing whatsoever, and condemned by the doctors who brought him into the world as a child who would have to go through life a deaf and dumb mute. Those were the words the doctors used; and when I heard those words, my very inner soul rebelled against them, and I said to myself and to those doctors, "My son may have been brought into the world without ears, but he is not going through life a deaf and dumb mute." That was my definite major purpose, ladies and gentlemen, the greatest I ever expect to have—far greater than my definite major purpose inaugurated by Andrew Carnegie when he selected me to start this philosophy destined to help millions of people throughout the world. That was not so great as my definite major purpose to force Nature to correct a mistake she had made in the birth of my son.

I went to work on it immediately. Of course, there was no way of reaching his consciousness by word, but I started in immediately, giving instructions to his subconscious mind in definite simple words, talking to him, and those instructions were for the subconscious mind to build a mechanism by which he could hear. I didn't tell Nature how to do this. I simply told Nature to do it and kept on for nine continuous years, day and night.

A definite major purpose is bound to bring results if the thing you are demanding is within the bounds of reason. By the age of three years, I had so alerted the child's mind that I could speak to him at his crib and wake him up immediately, even though he could not hear me. And then I began to work on him until, by the end of the ninth year, I had forced Nature to build a set of nerves to his brain through the skull so that he could hear through what is now known as bond induction.

And by that means he developed 65 percent of normal hearing, and with the aid of a hearing aid we provided the rest of it so that my son did not go through life a deaf and dumb mute. He would have if his father had not had the willpower to stay on the job and force Nature to correct the mistake.

That's the greatest thing I know of in my entire experience where the law of physical heredity has been called on to correct its mistake which it has made in connection with the physical body. I think perhaps not in the entire history of the medical profession will you find a case like my son, Blair. He not only hears as well as anybody, but he hears some sounds that you and I can't hear, especially the higher vibrations. And his sixth sense, his ability to pick up knowledge from Infinite Intelligence, is far greater than mine, and I have been using mine for the last 39 years, which shows that Nature, when you really go after her in the right way, will compensate for her mistakes in every way that she can.

I now want to call your attention to some outstanding people who have become so because of their understanding of the law of Cosmic Habit Force and their adaptation to it. When I say their understanding, I don't mean their conscious understanding; I mean the subconscious. And the first one is Henry Ford himself. I want you to study what happened in the case of Mr. Ford, a man without education, without financial backing.

He had very little opportunity to become anything except a farmer, and his father very probably wanted him to stay on the farm. He conceived an idea very early in life to the development and experimentation of which he devoted his entire life. I don't need to mention that idea. You know what it was as well as I do.

When he started out with the idea, from any angle of business or financial or economics that you might have chosen to analyze Mr. Ford, you would have said he hadn't a ghost of a chance to do what he set out to do. He became the greatest industrialist this country or any other country has ever produced. He became great—so great that money ceased to be of any concern to him one way or another. He built his entire worth starting from one simple idea and keeping on keeping on, and the thinking that kept him on the success beam was his knowledge. It might have been intuition or inspiration or something else, but he did have knowledge that there was a law which if you placed your mind on something definite and kept it there, this law could aid you in attaining the objective, whatever it might be.

In the beginning, he had every form of discouragement and public criticism. They even passed a police ordinance making it unlawful to operate his gadget on many streets—any street except the back streets—because it scared the horses. But the worst thing was the criticism of a great mass of people that went out against Henry Ford in the early days of the automobile. Nobody ever thought his automobile would start an industry except Henry Ford, but he kept on, kept his mind fixed on the idea, and eventually he forced the law of Cosmic Habit Force to make it so. He fixed it so definitely in his mind that the law couldn't get out of it, and then stumbling blocks became stepping-stones, disadvantages became opportunities. People, instead of criticizing him, wanted to help him, and the time came when they almost stood in line to invest money when he didn't need it.

What was it that made him the outstanding industrialist he was? Knowingly or not, he used the law of Cosmic Habit Force. That would apply, too, to Thomas A. Edison. He had little education, only three months, at the end of which a teacher sent him home with a note that said he had an addled brain and couldn't learn. On the way home he opened that note and read it and never told his parents, but he built up in his mind a resistance against that sort of condemnation that made him feel so humiliated, which made him look forward to the day when that teacher would eat crow. And fortunately, the teacher lived a long time and did apologize for discouraging him.

What happened to Edison was that as the result of that humiliation, he adopted a major purpose, and that changed from time to time; but what it began with was to show the world and that teacher and his parents that he did not have an addled mind, and I think he made a good job of it. If he did have an addled mind, I hope that I, too, have that same kind of an addled mind that he had.

It would have been following the line of least resistance and the natural thing to do, after he read that note, to throw it away or tear it up, say nothing about it to the parents, and build up a definite complex, a fixation of fear, based upon that indictment. That is what the average person probably would have done, but there must have been something in Mr. Edison's makeup that was not average. I don't know about that. I do know that he went into the business of inventing the incandescent light, and before he completed that he had more than 10,000 different failures. Can you imagine a person capable of turning on his willpower and staying behind a definite major purpose through 10,000 failures? If you can, you can imagine a genius like Mr. Edison was, and that was the thing that made him a genius. Ten thousand failures. The average person doesn't even fail one time before he quits because he anticipates failure first, sees it coming around the corner, and tucks his tail between his legs and runs.

I now wish to direct your attention to the most remarkable man it has ever been my privilege of knowing and working with. That man is the only one I have ever met who was able to form a direct contact with Infinite Intelligence and do his own Master Minding through his own brain without aligning himself with another in that Master Mind principle. That man is a man whom most of you have never heard of perhaps. He has been dead now almost 20 years. His name is Dr. Elmer R. Gates. His home was in Chevy Chase, Maryland. I had the privilege of working for three and a half years with Dr. Gates and with Dr. Alexander Graham Bell, the inventor of the long-distance telephone. Dr. Bell had developed, to a certain extent, the same ability that Dr. Gates had, and it was through this particular contact with Infinite Intelligence that he discovered the principle of the long-distance telephone.

I first met Dr. Gates when I was sent to him with a letter of introduction by Andrew Carnegie, who requested him to let me have the privilege of examining his scientific notes, particularly those that concerned metaphysics. Dr. Gates had done considerable experimenting in that field and had a very large number of notebooks on the subject of mind control, and mind discipline, and mind operation, all of which I had the privilege of examining. But the thing that interested me most about Dr. Gates was the method or technique through which he got information, facts, data, and directions from Infinite Intelligence.

Before I describe this method, I want to tell you what his theory was. His theory was that the thoughts of men and vibrations of thought released by men and women at certain high rates of vibration were picked up in the ether and controlled in the electrons and protons of matter, and that those thoughts remained in the outer ether and you could tune in on that ether under certain circumstances and pick up the thoughts of men released thousands or even millions of years ago. I recognize that this is a very deep subject. I saw a great deal of data in Dr. Elmer Gates's possession that convinced me that his theory was not far-fetched, and I saw him make demonstrations in his laboratory that were almost conclusive that the theory was not far-fetched.

When I got to his office the first time, I presented my letter of introduction, and the secretary said, "I'm sorry you will not be able to see Dr. Gates for almost three hours; he is sitting for ideas." I said, "Well, what does that mean?" She said, "I can't answer that for you; you will have to put that question to Dr. Gates and let him explain." I cooled my feet in the outer office for over three hours, and finally he came out. I presented my letter and told him what his secretary had said, and he said, "Would you like to see me sit for ideas?" I said, "I most certainly would."

He took me back to his laboratory, to a room ten by twelve feet, and there was nothing in it but a little wooden table with a pad and a pencil and a chair, and over the top of the table an electric push button to turn off and on the lights. That was where he sat for his ideas, and he explained that when he was in the business of wanting an invention or wanting an answer and didn't have it, he took the known part, the known facts, and went into his sound-proof room, switched off the lights so no influence could reach him, turned his attention to his sixth sense, and demanded that the unknown factor, X, would be revealed to him. While he was sitting, he said that oftentimes the information would start coming over instantaneously, and he would switch on the lights and start writing. On one occasion he wrote for almost three hours, and when he finished and examined his notes he had a great amount of data and he had the answer to one problem that had baffled the scientists down through the ages.

I am talking to you, ladies and gentlemen, about a great scientist, not a crackpot, and I am free to say to you that if I were in your place, I would at least say it was too deep for me if I had not seen it. But I was there, and I studied him for three and a half years, sufficient to convince me that there is a way to concentrate your mind on a definite major purpose until Nature is forced to yield up to you the means of attaining that purpose. I am truly confident of that.

He often went down to the Patent Office, and when he came across a patent which had been filed by somebody which he recognized to represent only the theory but not the practice—that is to say, the patent called for something that was theoretical only and not yet perfected— he would take a copy, go back to his sound-proof room, concentrate on the known factor, and demand that the unknown factor be revealed, or that the weakness be revealed. And by that method he completed and perfected over 350 patents during his lifetime, taking patents that wouldn't work and making them into something that would work. In other words, a lot of people who filed for patents had theoretical ideas but not the practical knowledge with which to make that idea work. Dr. Gates acquired the knowledge with which to make those patents workable and acquired it by dealing directly with the source of Infinite Intelligence, wherein is stored all the facts and all the knowledge available to mankind in the past, in the present, and for all I know, in the future.

There is a strange thing about this business of being able to concentrate your mind on what you want and keeping it focused on what you want until eventually you reach the point where it seems that everything you touch lends itself to help you acquire that which you want. One of the most difficult things for a student of this philosophy to do is to adopt a definite major purpose and keep the mind fixed upon that purpose with the intensity that I have described.

I want to tell you how the majority of my students operate, and this is no reflection on my students. They represent a cross-section of humanity. They all operate the same way. They start out by writing out a description of their definite major purpose, and a very favorite sum for them to put down is $100,000. I don't know why they use that so often, but they do. They will be very definite about this, and they usually want it within five years—about $20,000 a year. But when they get down to a description of what they have to offer in return for the $100,000, I discover that by no stretch of the imagination have they brought in enough to justify their getting that. And then, when they get on to step three and get to the plan, I find this plan to be very weak and oftentimes impractical. Then, when I come into contact with the student himself, I find out that instead of fixing the idea of his definite major purpose in his mind with the determination he will get the object no matter how long it will take, he has put it on paper with the hope that by some miracle the objective will reveal itself of its own accord and dump things into his front yard. That is the weakness of the average student in following instructions. He is not learning to intensify his desire until Cosmic Habit Force picks up those desires and acts upon them.

Now I want to call your attention to the difference between an ordinary desire and a burning desire. I had a burning desire to force Nature to develop a set of hearing aids for my son, and I kept on the job until Nature did just that. That was so burning that it became an obsession with me. I would have paid any price to carry out the objective of that desire.

A burning desire is one wherein you have hypnotized yourself so definitely that you can see yourself already in possession of the object of that desire even before you start acquiring it. That is self-hypnosis. Do you think it is a dangerous word? If you do, perish the idea, because you are using it every day whether you know it or not. The majority of people go all the way through life under the influence of self-hypnosis, by which they have released poverty-stricken or sick or ill-health thoughts. I have never yet found an outstanding man or woman in any calling that didn't have the power of instantaneous self-hypnosis. If you look up a great teacher, a great salesman, or anybody else, you will find a man who can very easily throw himself into the state of self-hypnosis back of any idea he chooses. But most people, instead of immunizing themselves to misfortunes, throw themselves on the opposite side by expecting them and finding them.

> *A burning desire is one wherein you have hypnotized yourself so definitely that you can see yourself already in possession of the object of that desire even before you start acquiring it.*

There are a great many things I might say to you over which I would admit that I am very proud, but there is one that stands out over all the others combined, and that is the statement that by the application of my own philosophy, I have put myself in the position where I don't fear anything in the world—this world or any other world—nothing at all. I haven't always been that way. There were times when I feared a great many things, and usually the things that I feared came upon me one way or the other. That was when I didn't understand the working of the law of Cosmic Habit Force. I want to tell you, all my freedom of body and freedom of mind came ten years ago when this law of Cosmic Habit Force was revealed to me for the first time; and incidentally, the desire had been in my mind a great many years to discover what was missing that made this philosophy impracticable and inactive at certain times. I knew there was a missing link, and just right at this time this law of Cosmic Habit Force was revealed.

I was visiting in the mountains of Virginia, and a policeman from Detroit was there. He was a retired policeman by the name of Roy S. Baker. He had been a policeman his entire life, was not educated, murdered the King's English when he spoke, and his manners were exceedingly bad. He was not a man to be greatly admired, but he did a very great thing for me for which I will always be thankful. He picked up one of the copies of *The Law of Success* books, thumbed through it for a few moments, threw it down, and said, "My friend, you have to dig further. You haven't got the last word in this philosophy yet." I remember so well what my reaction was—the same as yours would have been, perhaps. It was this: *How in the world would you be able to judge that philosophy with your lack of background and your ill manners? How would you be able to tell me what's missing?* But back of it all I recognized he was speaking the truth, and that very day I made a super effort, an effort such as I had never made before. I will not call it an effort but a demand upon my subconscious mind to go through instantly and find that missing link. And there was not a day after that until the law of Cosmic Habit Force was revealed that I didn't revitalize that determination. I didn't even know what I was searching for; but I did know what I wanted, and I was determined to get it.

When the revelation came, it came almost instantaneously as the result of one of the worst business experiences I have ever had in my life. And in the middle of this experience, things became so confused, I said, "I am going to take today off and let my mind rest and clear my mind." And I got into my car and drove to the State of New Jersey. I went to a spot where nobody could reach me by telephone. I just wanted to get away and give my mind a little rest. And do you know that on the way over there, before I reached my destination, my mind had commenced to tune in on the law of Cosmic Habit Force?

And when it came to me, I called it the wrong name. I called it the law of hypnotic rhythm. When I came back to New York and presented this to my great friend and advisor, Francis I. Hubaugh, he instantly said, "You have come upon a great law that may be of more importance to humanity than anything Einstein has discovered in relativity, but you have given it the wrong name, the negative name. It would be the law of hypnotic rhythm in the negative, when you allow your mind to dwell on poverty and ill health and defeat and then nature applies the law of hypnotic rhythm and fixes them on you, carries them out." Mr. Hubaugh said, "What you really want to do is give that law a positive name," and we sat there and talked about it. And I said, "As a matter of fact, it is cosmic, a law that controls the physical universe and is the fixer of all habits," and I said, "I have the name now—the law of Cosmic Habit Force." And he said, "That's perfect—that's the perfect application of this great law, the law of Cosmic Habit Force, through which when you repeat an idea over and over it is picked up and made into a mental record, so to speak, the needle of thought drops into that groove and begins to turn automatically, and whatever the nature of that groove it becomes deeper and deeper, and Cosmic Habit Force works on the ideas while you sleep."

I recognize that you and I are workaday folks. We don't aspire to become great scientists. We just want to get through life with peace of mind and good health and the things we need. But no matter what our aspirations may be, we need to recognize that we haven't learned yet the last word in the control of the mind. We haven't learned the first word.

In our own public school system, we study almost everything else. Perhaps it would be better if we were taught nothing in the public school system that is now taught and instead were taught to turn our attention within and find out what causes us to think as we do, what forms and enables out habits, and what goes on in the human mind.

I can appreciate what Plato had in mind when he forced his students to study and analyze the bones of a frog's head. It wasn't the frog's head he was so interested in. He wanted them to learn the law of concentration. Students of the law of Cosmic Habit Force, students of this philosophy who learn to apply the law of Cosmic Habit Force, will learn that they can expect greater things than anything they ever imagined. They will have no difficulty in acquiring all the things in life they want and need. They can voluntarily put in the mind any idea they want to keep and bring it back until it is taken over by Cosmic Habit Force, and then they will have done the things that our conscious minds call genius through their achievement.

We have come to the end of our final lesson. Please use what you have learned to attain understanding, success, and peace of mind.

AFTERWORD

The Importance of Annie Lou, Napoleon Hill's Last Wife

By Don M. Green

Annie Lou's support of Napoleon Hill started in the early 1940s, and her dedication to him and his work continued into the 1950s. In 1952, Napoleon Hill started a business relation with W. Clement Stone to promote the principles of success. Hill and Stone had definite objectives in mind. First, they wanted to spread the philosophy of success to as many people as possible. The second goal was to develop programs to create profits to get the enterprise to be self-sufficient and self-perpetuating so that the teaching of Hill's philosophy would continue even after Hill and Stone were no longer alive. Annie Lou was always a clear thinker, and her companionship and organizational skills were vital to what Hill and Stone were creating for the future.

Annie Lou also never let Napoleon lose sight of friends and family as being the most important things in their life. Napoleon many times neglected family and friends in pursuit of dreams he chased during his early life. He had three sons by Florence, whose 25-year marriage to him ended due to his neglect of her and the boys. Early in their marriage, Annie Lou corresponded with his sons, and they were able to exchange letters and even schedule visits. It was a much better relationship than Hill had enjoyed in many years. The relationship was never what could be considered normal between father and sons, but Annie Lou had removed the hatred between them.

In August 1962, Napoleon and Annie Lou signed the articles of incorporation for their new Napoleon Hill Foundation. The nonprofit Napoleon Hill Foundation owes its existence to the desire to promote personal achievements in people's lives. The Foundation originally consisted of only three officers and trustees: Napoleon Hill, Annie Lou Hill, and Hill's attorney.

With a small office in Columbia, South Carolina, the work of the Foundation began. It developed an agenda focused on prison rehabilitation programs, an international leadership school, and a national franchise program that would teach, train, and license individual entrepreneurs to market its courses and literature for a profit.

When Napoleon approached his last years, he wanted two things, the first being that Annie Lou be financially secure and second that his work be spread throughout the world forever by the Napoleon Hill Foundation that he and Annie Lou had founded. Annie Lou was left in excellent financial shape when Hill died in 1970. She was left an estate that made her a millionaire, so her finances were well taken care of. Napoleon died at the age of 87, and Annie Lou was nearly 80.

Annie Lou lived 14 more years after Napoleon died, and she maintained a treasury of material that is now a part of the Napoleon Hill Foundation archives. The valuable collection has been shared and will continue to be shared with Napoleon Hill followers by the Foundation, which now, more than a half century after its founding, continues to spread the teachings of the science of personal achievement so well developed and documented by Napoleon Hill.

About Napoleon Hill

Napoleon Hill was born in 1883 in a one-room cabin on the Pound River in Wise County, Virginia. He began his writing career at age 13 as a "mountain reporter" for small town newspapers and went on to become America's most beloved motivational author. Hill passed away in November 1970 after a long and successful career writing, teaching, and lecturing about the principles of success. Dr. Hill's work stands as a monument to individual achievement and is the cornerstone of modern motivation. His book, *Think and Grow Rich*, is the all-time best-seller in the field. Hill established the Foundation as a nonprofit educational institution whose mission is to perpetuate his philosophy of leadership, self-motivation, and individual achievement. His books, audio cassettes, videotapes, and other motivational products are made available to you as a service of the Foundation so that you may build your own library of personal achievement materials...and help you acquire financial wealth and the true riches of life.

The purpose of The Napoleon Hill Foundation is to…

- *Advance the concept of private enterprise offered under the American System*
- *Teach individuals by formula how they can rise from humble beginnings to positions of leadership in their chosen professions*
- *Assist young men and women to set goals for their own lives and careers*
- *Emphasize the importance of honesty, morality and integrity as the cornerstone of Americanism*
- *Aid in the development of individuals to help them reach their own potential*
- *Overcome the self-imposed limitations of fear, doubt and procrastination*
- *Help people rise from poverty, physical handicaps, and other disadvantages to high positions, wealth and acquisition of the true riches of life*
- *Motivate individuals to motivate themselves to high achievements*

The Napoleon Hill Foundation
www.naphill.org

A not-for-profit educational institution dedicated
to making the world a better place in which to live.

TO CLAIM YOUR ADDITIONAL FREE RESOURCES PLEASE VISIT
SOUNDWISDOM.COM/NAPHILL

AN OFFICIAL PUBLICATION OF
THE NAPOLEON HILL FOUNDATION

GET YOUR COPY TODAY!
AVAILABLE EVERYWHERE BOOKS ARE SOLD

www.ingramcontent.com/pod-product-compliance
Lightning Source LLC
Chambersburg PA
CBHW060518100426
42743CB00009B/1364